THE PRODUCE COMPANION

THE
PRODUCE
COMPANION

From balconies to backyards,
the complete guide to growing,
pickling and preserving

MEREDITH KIRTON & MANDY SINCLAIR

hardie grant books

CONTENTS

RECIPES

INTRODUCTION

There's nothing quite like the satisfaction you get from growing and preserving your own produce.

These practices have waned over the years, however it is with much joy that both are returning in earnest as we rediscover the health benefits and economic value of consuming home-grown food, and we begin to understand that supermarket convenience isn't the be-all and end-all.

With Meredith a gardener and Mandy a passionate foodie, neither of us can bear waste, and we appreciate more than most the toil that goes into producing. It seems so ungrateful not to make use of everything. Even scraps become compost and in turn, rich food for another crop. So it makes perfect sense to preserve one's harvest.

When thinking of preserving, most people's minds go directly to bottles of beautiful fruit, delicious jams and pungent chutneys, but preserving can be much more than this. Within this book you will also find pestos, flavoured butters, fruit curds and simple sorbets. Detailed gardening information gives you tips for getting your produce growing well, plus plenty of ideas for things to do with your crop – from the basics of freezing and drying, to sun-drying summer fruit, candying citrus peel, drying tomato skins to make a paprika-like powder, and even smoking chillies and garlic.

During the journey of writing this book, it was wonderful to discover that preserving isn't just about the long-term benefits – it's also about the flavour of the end product and the joy the whole process evokes. The smell of cooking with spices like cloves, cinnamon and star anise or just the simple fragrance of citrus simmering is always a delight. Seeing light shining through your intensely coloured bottles of preserves like stained glass, and having a shelf stocked with homemade goodies, can't help but create a sense of happiness. It feels so comforting to know there is something for a rainy day, a quiet indulgence or a gift for a loved friend.

The process of trying to use everything and waste little has led to many a taste sensation. Green oranges, for example, removed from a tree that needed pruning, proved to make the most incredible zesty syrup. In the same vein our grandparents often preserved green peaches before any spoiling from fruit fly could occur, and these too had a wonderful tartness that was unique and delicious.

We hope that this book will inspire you to turn a garden glut into a bounty worth sharing, hoarding and treasuring.

PRESERVING KNOW-HOW

Generally speaking, preserving your own produce is a straightforward process – but it must be said that it isn't always foolproof.

Embracing preserving at home means you may have the occasional failure. The key is to learn from failures by understanding the problem and how to prevent it from happening next time. Even then, you may not have success each and every time, as I have learnt during my journey.

This section gives you some guidelines to help increase your success rate, and to help identify what to do differently next time in the case of failure.

SPOILAGE

Spoilage occurs when there is the presence of bacteria, mould, yeasts or enzymes. Identifying spoiled food may seem obvious, however due to our lives being dominated by the supermarket, few of us have had the experience of opening a tin or jar of preserved food that has spoiled.

Identifying spoiled food

→ Use your senses – the preserve should look and smell the same as when you bottled it.
→ If you see mould or if the contents fizz when you unscrew the lid – even if it smells normal – the preserve should be discarded.
→ If the lid has popped or you can see bubbles in the liquid, discard the preserve.

→ If produce that has been preserved whole or in large pieces feels soft and slimy, discard it.
→ If in doubt, don't consume – it just isn't worth a bout of food poisoning.

Ways to prevent spoilage

→ Sterilise everything that comes into contact with the preserve after it has finished cooking – jars or bottles, lids, seals, ladles, tongs, funnels, jugs, cloths for wiping. See page 10 for sterilising methods.
→ Ensure that you bottle your jams, chutneys and other similar preserves while they are hot, using freshly sterilised, still-warm jars, and seal with the lids immediately. This creates a vacuum seal in the jars as the contents cool down, which sucks the lids down firmly and excludes air.
→ Preserves that do not contain high amounts of sugar or acid need to be heat-processed (see page 12). Heat-processing also creates a vacuum seal.
→ Ensure sterilised jars or bottles are dry before filling.
→ Wash, peel and blanch fruit and vegetables where possible.
→ Use fresh, unblemished produce – starting with perfect produce will help to create perfect preserves.

- → Ensure you use the correct amount of sugar or vinegar stated in the recipe.
- → While there is no scientific evidence to support this, I always wipe down the tops of my sealed jars or bottles with eucalyptus or tea-tree oil as an extra precaution. This is something my grandmother always did, and so I have continued with it.
- → If re-using lids, ensure there is no damage or obvious rust on the underside. If using purpose-made preserving jars or bottles, it is best to use new lids and bands for each re-use of the jar or bottle.
- → When preserving in salt, use plastic-lined lids to prevent corrosion.
- → When freezing produce in zip-lock bags, remove as much air as possible before sealing the bag. Try using a straw to suck excess air out.
- → Store dried fruit and vegetables in a jar or airtight container, but check after a week to make sure there is no condensation inside. If there is, dry the fruit or vegetable a little longer.

STERILISING

- → While it is perfectly okay to re-use jars, they must be in good condition, especially the lids. Scrape off any old labels and glue, wash well in hot soapy water and rinse off the suds.
- → To sterilise jars in the oven, place jars upside down on a tray lined with a clean cloth or on a rack and put them in an oven heated to 120°C (250°F) for 10 minutes.
- → If you have a steam oven, place jars upside down on a rack and steam at 100°C (210°F) for 15 minutes. Place on a clean tea towel to dry.
- → To sterilise jars by boiling, stand jars upright on a rack or trivet in the base of a deep pot. Fill the jars and pot with warm water, ensuring the jars are covered, and bring to the boil. Simmer for 10 minutes. Use tongs to carefully remove the jars and tip out the water inside, and place upside down on a clean tea towel to dry.
- → To sterilise lids, boil them for 10 minutes. Remove from the water and place on a clean tea towel to drain.
- → To sterilise funnels, ladles, tongs, cloths for wiping and other equipment, boil them for 5 minutes.
- → Always have your jars or bottles (and lids) ready to be filled as soon as the cooking is finished. Ensure the jars are still warm as there is a risk of cracking when ladling hot jam into cold jars.
- → Have a damp sterilised cloth on hand to wipe down any spills around jars if needed.

HEAT-PROCESSING

Heat-processing or water-bathing extends the shelf life of preserves, and is particularly relevant to low-acid foods and recipes without much sugar or vinegar.

Use preserving jars that have 2-part lids – a flat disc and a screw band that goes over the top. Sterilise the jars and lids and fill them with your preserve, leaving headroom of 2 cm (¾ in) to allow for expansion. Stand the jars on a rack or trivet in the base of a deep pot. Wind a tea towel around the jars to prevent them touching while boiling. Add boiling water to the pot (if the contents of the jars are hot – otherwise start with cold or warm water), covering the jars by at least 3 cm (1¼ in). Put on a tight-fitting lid and simmer for 20 minutes – or longer for some recipes, where specified.

After boiling, remove the jars to a wooden board and leave to cool.

JAM-MAKING

Pectin

Pectin is necessary when making jams. It is a natural substance found in fruit and is released when the fruit is cooked with the correct amount of sugar and acid (such as lemon juice), which together react to set the jam. Different fruits have different pectin levels. Here are a few tips towards understanding pectin:

→ Underripe fruit has higher levels of pectin.
→ Pectin levels decrease the longer fruit is stored, so use recently harvested fruit if possible.

→ When using low-pectin fruit, consider mixing it with high-pectin fruit.
→ Acid helps to release pectin, hence the addition of lemon juice, particularly in recipes with low-pectin fruit.
→ Pectin is highest in the skin and seeds of fruit. Adding a muslin (cheesecloth) bag of lemon skins, pith and seeds will help to increase pectin levels as well as acid levels.

Pectin levels in fruit

LOW	MEDIUM	HIGH
cherries	apples	citrus fruits
elderberries	apricots	crab-apples
figs	blackberries	grapes
guavas	plums	mangoes
nectarines	raspberries	papayas
passionfruit	rosellas	quinces
peaches		
pears		
pineapples		
rhubarb		
rockmelons		
strawberries		
watermelons		

More jam-making tips

→ To avoid crystallisation, make sure the sugar has fully dissolved into the fruit before the jam comes to the boil, stirring it over low heat. Afterwards, you can increase the heat. I use caster (superfine) sugar throughout the book as its fine texture dissolves faster than regular granulated sugar. By all means use granulated sugar if you prefer – just be sure to stir over low heat until dissolved.
→ Most jams will need skimming during cooking to remove foam released from the

fruit, as this would also settle on top of your jars of jam. Use a large spoon to scoop it off the surface.

→ You can test for setting with a candy thermometer – when the mixture reaches 105°C (220°F), the jam is at setting point. Alternatively, place a small plate into the freezer until cold. Drop a teaspoon of jam onto the plate and leave to cool, returning it to the freezer for a couple of minutes if desired. The jam should appear firm with a wrinkle on the surface. You can also tilt the plate or run your finger through the jam to check its consistency.

MORE PRESERVING WISDOM

→ Always label and date your preserves.
→ Store in a cool, dark place and refrigerate after opening.
→ Chutneys and pickles are at their best from about 4 weeks after bottling. The flavours will mellow and become less 'vinegary'.

→ When straining jellies, use a square of muslin (cheesecloth) over a fine-mesh sieve. An alternative to muslin is a Chux cloth.

→ Sugar syrups are referred to as light, medium or heavy. A light syrup is made with 200 g (7 oz) of sugar dissolved in 1 litre (34 fl oz/4 cups) of water (a ratio of 1:5).
A medium syrup is 400 g (14 oz) of sugar to 1 litre (34 fl oz/4 cups) of water (2:5).
A heavy syrup is equal sugar to water (1:1).

→ Citrus fruit in particular benefits from a good wash before using to remove any scale or sprays that may have been used. If scale is hard to remove, try rubbing it with an oiled cloth.

→ Before preparing vegetables such as broccoli, cauliflower and cabbage, give them a soak in salted water for about 30 minutes to bring out any hidden bugs.

APPLES

 ## GROWING

Apples prefer a cool temperate climate and are adaptable to various soils and pH levels, though they do like regular deep waterings. They tend to produce suckers from the base, so be careful to remove these as low down as possible each year, along with any diseased or inward growth. Apples generally need another variety planted nearby for pollination, so multi-grafted apples are popular – though crab-apples can also be planted nearby for this purpose. Jonathan and golden delicious are partially self-fertile but will bear heavier crops with another type nearby.

Apples are small trees growing to about 4 x 4 m (13 x 13 ft). They have delightful blossoms in spring and start cropping after 3 years, coming into proper production after 5 years and continuing until they are about 30 years old. They bear fruit from summer to late autumn, depending on the variety. Some of the best early apples are royal gala and gravenstein, while pink lady, sundowner, fuji and granny smith are better mid-season or late-season apples.

Codling moth is a problem with apples as their larvae bury into the fruit. You can successfully regulate using pheromone ties that prevent male and female moths from finding each other, stopping the females from laying any eggs.

 ## HARVESTING

Check the colour of the inward-facing side of your apples – when this has changed colour, your apples should be ripe. The apples should come away easily from the tree with a gentle twist, and another way to check is to cut an apple to see if its seeds have turned brown.

A whole apple tree doesn't spontaneously ripen, but rather gives you many weeks of continuous cropping with the sunniest side ripening first, so you can pick over a tree many times. When picking your apples, try and leave the stem intact as they store better this way.

STORING

Store apples in a cool, dark place such as a garage, away from any potatoes. The specially made cardboard trays with a hollow for each apple that you may have seen at greengrocers are perfect for storing apples. They keep each one separate so that one rotten apple doesn't spoil the whole lot, or the whole barrel, as the saying goes. Without these trays, you can wrap apples in tissue paper or newspaper before putting them in a box, or store them on wooden trays with space in between to allow for air movement. Jonathan and golden delicious apples keep for 3 months; spartan keep for 4 months.

See recipes on pages 167, 172, 225, 243, 269 and 338

APRICOTS

☀ GROWING

Apricots are a cool-climate fruit that like a full-sun position with well-drained, organically enriched soil, and a neutral to slightly alkaline pH. They like a long, dry spring, but because they have a shallow root system they are particularly vulnerable to drying out. For this reason, make sure your tree is mulched and regularly watered, particularly in dry spells or when bearing fruit. Feed it with complete plant food in spring.

Apricots are a small tree growing to around 4 x 4 m (13 x 13 ft), and they are self-fertile (though they need bees to pollinate them), normally living for about 3 decades. They start bearing fruit after 2 years, though will fruit properly from about 6 years old. Frost can damage the blossoms, so apricots are sometimes grown against a sunny wall that radiates warmth throughout the night and prevents frost damage. Alternatively, a screen made by hammering stakes into the ground around the tree and wrapping with shade cloth or hessian can be put up when the tree is in blossom. This needs to be replaced with bird netting some months later when the apricots start to colour – it should go over the whole tree and be tied beneath the branches to be most effective. Heavy crops of apricots should be thinned out when the fruits are about the size of marbles, making sure there is enough space for each one to grow.

Apricots have a small harvest window of usually about 3 weeks per tree, which makes a freshly picked apricot something of a treat. However, different varieties ripen at different times from late spring to mid-summer. The best flavour comes from fruit that is allowed to fully ripen on the tree to become fragrant, sweet and soft. You will first see apricots change colour from green to yellowish orange, and then deepen in colour depending on the variety. Use delicate hands when harvesting as apricots bruise easily, and they are also best picked with their stalks still on as this helps them keep as long as possible.

STORING

Storing fresh apricots is difficult. They need to be completely bruise free and in a single layer. Even then, 1–3 weeks in a cool, well-ventilated place is all the shelf life you can expect. For this reason apricots are well suited to preserving, freezing and drying.

To freeze apricots, blanch them for 30 seconds then plunge them into iced water to refresh them. This brief cooking prevents their skins from toughening in the freezer. Prepare a bowl of water with a few vitamin C tablets (ascorbic acid) added. Halve and stone the apricots and soak them in the water for 5 minutes, which prevents them browning. After draining they can be frozen on a tray lined with baking paper – when hard, pack into zip-lock bags removing as much air as possible. Alternatively, they can be puréed, immersed in

syrup made with 1 part sugar to 2 parts water, or sprinkled in a sugar mix (145 g/5 oz/⅔ cup of sugar and ¼ teaspoon of ascorbic acid) and frozen in airtight containers. Apricots will keep in the freezer for up to 12 months.

To dry apricots, soak them as above. If using an oven, preheat it to its lowest temperature with the fan on. Place the halved fruit skin-side down on wire racks set on trays. Leave the door open slightly and dry for about 24 hours, until there is no visible moisture left in the fruit but it is still pliable. Leave to cool in the oven. In hot weather apricots can also be dried on a table in the sun, but care needs to be taken that the fruit is covered with muslin (cheesecloth) so that bugs and dirt don't land on the fruit. Placing the legs of the table in saucers of water can stop insects from crawling up from the ground. The fruit should be left out in hot sunshine for 3–4 days, but brought in at night. Store apricots in a jar, but check after a week to make sure there is no condensation. If there is, dry the apricots a little longer. Dried apricots should keep for up to 6 months in a cool, dark place; 12 months in the refrigerator; or 2 years in the freezer.

See recipes on pages 268 and 284

BLUEBERRIES

 ## GROWING

Blueberries are an attractive plant with their soft grey-green leaves, which in some varieties put on a colourful autumn display. In spring the plants have white bell-shaped flowers. They are a medium-sized shrub, growing around 2 m (6½ ft) tall, and like an acidic, free-draining soil and shelter from strong winds. There are many varieties, some tolerating frost and others even suited to the subtropics. Individual plants produce around 3 kg (6½ lb) of berries each year.

After a blueberry bush has been established for about 3 years, it needs to be pruned judiciously by removing old wood from the base at the end of winter, before new growth appears – this encourages new fruit-bearing shoots and keeps the bush from becoming too dense. Blueberries can also be tip-pruned throughout the year to encourage new growth. Netting to keep out the birds is essential, and a fine muslin (cheesecloth) throw is perfect for the job; it can be held into place with clothes pegs.

 ## HARVESTING

Ripe blueberries will easily pull from the bush, and should be soft with a waxy bloom on the skin. The deeper the colour, the sweeter the blueberry.

 ## STORING

Freshly picked blueberries will keep at a cool room temperature for 5 days, or in the refrigerator for up to 3 weeks. They can be frozen on a tray lined with baking paper – once hard, pack them into zip-lock bags removing as much air as possible. Frozen blueberries will last in the freezer for up to 12 months.

See recipe on page 282

CHERRIES

☀ GROWING

Cherries need a chilly winter to go into proper dormancy, after which they can burst into blossom and new growth and produce plenty of fruit. Their spring blossoms are among the prettiest of all fruit tree flowers. They hang down daintily on their long cherry stems, lasting a few weeks. Depending on the variety and climate, cherries fruit from mid-spring to late summer. Luckily for gardeners, cherry trees keep on giving in the garden as in autumn they have a lovely foliage display, and their wonderfully gnarled branching is shown off in winter when the trees are bare.

Grow cherries in a position that is sunny but with some protection from hot summer winds. They like well-drained, slightly acidic soil and deep summer soakings, though too much rain in spring can cause the fruit to split. Feed annually with complete plant food, and prune in winter to an open vase shape and manageable harvest height, removing any diseased wood at the same time.

Cherries mostly need another variety planted nearby for pollination, although some such as stella, sunburst and starkrimson are self-fertile. They should start to crop after about 3 years, and be in full production after 6 years, lasting for the next 3 or 4 decades. Birds love cherries, so always net your trees as the fruit starts to ripen or you might miss out on a worthwhile harvest. Pear and cherry slug can be a problem – see Pears, page 49.

🐦 HARVESTING

Cherries are best picked when they are uniform in colour and have shiny skin. Simply pinch them off holding the stalk between your thumb and forefinger using a twisting action. Be careful not to remove the bud that the cherry came from, as next year's crop will come from the same buds. Place your picked cherries in a shallow bucket, being careful not to bruise them.

☰ STORING

Cherries with their stalk attached can be placed in a plastic bag, or loosely packed in a container, and stored in the refrigerator for up to 1 week.

To freeze cherries, stone them using a cherry or olive stoner and pack them into zip-lock bags, or place in an airtight container and cover in a sugar syrup made with 1 part sugar to 2 parts water, and store in the freezer for up to 12 months.

Cherries can also be stewed, made into syrups and jams, glacéd and crystallised. Making glacé cherries is an interesting process that basically involves replacing the water inside a cherry with sugar via daily dousings of syrup, which gets increasingly more sugary over the course of a fortnight.

To make glacé cherries, stone 500 g (1 lb 2 oz) of cherries using a cherry or olive stoner. Place them in a bowl and cover with

600 ml (20 fl oz) of boiling water and leave to soak until just soft. Drain, reserving the water, and transfer the cherries to a medium-sized bowl or dish. Pour 425 ml (14 fl oz) of the soaking water into a saucepan and add 250 g (9 oz) of caster (superfine) sugar. Heat gently, stirring until the sugar dissolves, then pour on top of the cherries. Cover and leave to steep overnight. The next day, strain the syrup into a saucepan and add another 70 g (2½ oz) of caster sugar. Heat gently, stirring, until the sugar dissolves, and return to the cherries. Repeat for another 6 days, adding extra sugar to the syrup daily. After this, add 85 g (3 oz) of caster sugar to the syrup and leave the cherries to steep for 2 days. Repeat, but this time leave to steep for 4 days. The cherries should now be ready to place on a wire rack to dry. Store them in a sterilised jar in a cool, dark place for up to 12 months.

See recipe on page 342

CITRUS

☀ GROWING

Citrus are perfect backyard trees with their fragrant blossom, evergreen foliage and attractive winter fruits. They grow in many climates except where winters are very cold – but if potted, citrus can see the winter through in a glasshouse (or traditionally in an orangery), or just in a bright sunroom. The varieties that are most tolerant of cold include the cumquat, seville orange, mandarin and meyer lemon (a less acidic and more orange-coloured lemon than the lisbon or the eureka).

Citrus like a rich, slightly acidic soil that drains well and a sunny position. Care needs to be taken to remove low-hanging branches (called 'lifting the crown') so that air can flow around the trees, ensuring they don't get collar rot. You should also remove any swollen stems in winter as these are caused by the citrus gall wasp.

Feed citrus regularly with a combination of citrus fertiliser and pelletised manure, and use an oil-based spray throughout spring, summer and early autumn to help control pests such as aphids, scale, leafminer and bronze orange bug. Crops should be thinned, especially when the trees are young, so that branches don't break under the weight. If you are thinning oranges, you might consider using rather than discarding your green oranges as they have their own unique scent and flavour (see Green-orange syrup, page 165).

✈ HARVESTING

Different citrus trees have different ripening styles. Mandarins and limes tend to have a shorter harvesting window, whereas eureka and lisbon lemons can be held on the tree for months, and navel oranges actually sweeten if left on the tree until after the first frost. Most citrus fruit should remain on the tree until it is fully coloured, apart from limes, which should be picked before they turn yellow and drop.

When harvesting citrus fruit, don't just pull the fruit off the branch, because when the stem comes out it leaves a small hole. This is fine if you're going to use the fruit immediately, but for storage you should avoid this wound that lets in fungi or bacteria and causes the fruit to rot. The solution is to use scissors to snip the fruit off the tree with some stem attached. The shelf life of the fruit can also be extended by not picking when it's particularly cold or wet.

≡ STORING

Citrus fruit should keep in a perforated plastic bag in the crisper for at least a month. If short of space, the alternative is packing them in a box with newspaper between the layers, or in dry sand, and storing in a well-ventilated, cool, dark place. The fruit should keep for many weeks, with lemons lasting the best this way.

Storing lemons actually increases their juiciness. Often when you pick and use a lemon

immediately, you find the pith is thick and there is little juice. Storing for at least a week reduces the thickness of the pith and gives you a lot more juice.

If you are using any citrus fruit whole or for its skin, you should give it a good wash first to remove any scale. If scale is hard to remove, try rubbing with an oiled cloth.

Lemons can also be frozen whole in bags for up to 6 months and then defrosted in cold water for 10 minutes before use. Alternatively, you can cut up wedges of lemon and freeze them in zip-lock bags, or squeeze lemon juice into ice-cube trays then transfer the cubes to zip-lock bags once frozen.

To make dehydrated lemon slices (or orange, grapefruit or lime slices), cut the fruit as thin as possible and place on trays lined with baking paper. Dry in an oven heated to its lowest temperature with the fan on and with the door slightly ajar. Flip the slices after about 2 hours and keep cooking until there is no moisture left in them. Leave the slices to cool in the oven. Store in a jar in a cool, dark place for up to 12 months. These slices can be used in flavoured teas or in soups, or blended into rubs for meat or seafood.

The peel of both mandarins and oranges can be candied (navel oranges are particularly fragrant) or dried in strips to add to stocks and stews. **To dry peel**, use a vegetable peeler to remove strips of rind with as little pith as possible. Place the strips in a single layer on a wire rack and leave at room temperature for a few days. Alternatively, the rind can be threaded onto cotton and hung as garlands to dry (you can even cut the rind into shapes with a cookie cutter). Once dry, store the rind in a jar in a cool, dark place for up to 12 months.

To candy citrus peel, use a vegetable peeler to remove strips of rind with as little pith as possible from about 6 oranges (or the equivalent

of any citrus fruit, even a mixture). Put in a saucepan with 190 ml (6½ fl oz/¾ cup) of water and ½ teaspoon of salt and bring to the boil. Simmer for 10 minutes, then drain and repeat in fresh salted water. Drain for a second time, then put 460 g (1 lb/2 cups) of caster (superfine) sugar into the saucepan with 500 ml (17 fl oz/2 cups) of water. Bring to the boil, stirring until the sugar has dissolved. Add the rind and simmer for 40–60 minutes, then lift from the syrup with a slotted spoon and place on lightly oiled baking paper. Once dry, store the peel in a sterilised jar in a cool, dark place for up to 12 months. You can use the peel in cakes, desserts or as a garnish, or dip it into chocolate as an after-dinner treat. You can also use the syrup like a cordial – just add soda water (club soda).

Cumquats are excellent for candying (see page 278) and are a traditional food of Chinese New Year – especially when made with the marumi variety. Cumquats are a symbol of prosperity and good luck.

Preserving lemons and other citrus fruit in salt is another great way of keeping them (see page 314). **To salt cumquats**, wash them and lay them out in the sun for a few days (bringing them in at night) until their skins wrinkle. Layer with generous salt in a sterilised jar with a plastic-lined lid (salt is corrosive to metal). Leave in a cool, dark place for at least 1 month, turning the cumquats over in the juice that the salt extracts every few days. You can add spices like bay leaves, thyme and cumin seeds. Use the cumquats whole or chopped in Chinese stews and soups, or add them to soda water (club soda) for a refreshing and therapeutic drink.

See recipes on pages 165, 170, 208, 251, 253, 272, 278, 310 and 314 .

CRAB-APPLES

GROWING

Crab-apples are the precursors to the modern apple. They have small, cherry-sized fruits that are hard and tart when ripe and come in a range of colours, from purple to yellow, orange, green and red. The trees tolerate a wide range of climates and soils, but prefer a chill over winter so they can set plenty of fruit. They are normally grown for their ornamental value – primarily their spring blossoms – but the 'crabs' are a useful (and attractive) bonus, appearing from summer through autumn. Partially self-fertile, crab-apples can also cross-pollinate other apples.

HARVESTING

Crab-apples are ripe when they are well coloured but still firm. Pick them with secateurs in clusters. The fruit holds well on the tree so you don't need to pick them immediately if it doesn't suit you.

STORING

Crab-apples can be stored in a box between layers of paper in a cool, dark place for a few weeks, or in a perforated plastic bag in the crisper for up to 2 months, until you're ready to use them. If you're making crab-apple jelly but don't want to do it straight away, then an even better storage idea is to boil the crab-apples to make a stock, then strain (discarding the apples) and freeze in an airtight container.

A lovely thing to add to crab-apple jelly is herbs such as rosemary, thyme, sage or mint. Stir in sprigs of your favourite herb after you have removed the jelly from the heat. Rosemary or thyme can be bottled with the jelly, while mint or sage should be left to infuse the jelly for 5 minutes before being removed. Herb-flavoured jelly is perfect for basting roast meats or deglazing a lamb or veal cutlet in a frying pan.

See recipes on pages 275 and 276

FIGS

 ## GROWING

Eat a fig still warm from the sun and it's easy to see how figs made it into the Garden of Eden! Figs will grow in any Mediterranean-style climate or warm temperate area, and even in colder areas if given a sheltered microclimate. The common varieties are self-fertile and can fruit twice a year, first in early summer, then with the bulk of fruit in early autumn, making them double value for the home gardener.

Birds love figs and they need to be netted. The trees can also get attacked by pink wax scale, which can be organically treated with white oil every month after it first appears. Mulch figs in winter and apply a few handfuls of blood and bone and complete plant food in spring. Figs can grow into large trees, and restricting the roots with a root control barrier can encourage heavier crops. The trees should start to bear in a few years; will produce well in about 7 years; and be bearing fully for another 40 years or so. Over-watering can cause the fruit to swell and split, though the trees do like to be kept moist. In colder areas you should protect young shoots from late frost, especially when the tree is young, by hammering stakes around the tree and wrapping with some shade cloth or hessian, or by throwing a large piece of the material over the whole tree and pegging it into place.

 ## HARVESTING

Figs need to be ripe when picked as they don't continue ripening afterwards. Their colour varies according to the variety, with some skins brown when ripe and others remaining green. You can tell that they are ripe when the fruit hangs down, the neck wilts, and their bases even start to split a little. You can smell the nectar of a ripe fig, too. Try to pick them with some stalk attached, using a sharp knife or scissors if needed.

STORING

Fresh figs bruise easily so should be handled with care. Make sure you keep them in a single layer, and keep them away from other fruits and vegetables. Eat within a few days. To keep figs longer either freeze or dry them, turn them into jam, or preserve your crop.

To freeze figs, place them on a tray lined with baking paper and when hard, pack them into zip-lock bags removing as much air as possible. They should keep for up to 12 months. When defrosted they can be used in jams, pastes and baking.

To dry figs, wash them, cut them in half lengthways and place them skin-side down on a wire rack. If the weather is right with several hot, dry and even windy days forecast, you can place them on a table, protect them with muslin (cheesecloth) and dry them outside in the

sun, bringing them in each night. Placing the legs of the table in saucers of water can stop insects from crawling up from the ground. If the weather is otherwise, place the figs in an oven preheated to its lowest temperature with the fan on and the door slightly ajar. Dry the figs for 8–12 hours, until there is no moisture left in the figs and they are leathery. Leave to cool in the oven.

Store the dried figs in a jar, but check after a week to make sure there is no condensation. If there is, dry the figs a little longer. Dried figs should keep for up to 6 months in a cool, dark place; 12 months in the refrigerator; or 2 years in the freezer.

See recipe on page 274

GUAVAS

☀ GROWING

Guavas range from the large apple variety to the small strawberry or cherry guava, to the medium-sized pineapple guava or feijoa. All usually grow into small trees 3–5 m (10–16 ft) tall and like well-drained, well-fed soil. They are prolific bearers, providing masses of autumn fruit (up to 100 kg/220 lb per tree per year) after about 4–5 years.

With the exception of the feijoa, these trees like a warm climate. The feijoa is actually a different species and can tolerate frost and also drought. It is quite a garden feature plant with stripy bark, red flowers and silvery foliage, and can even be hedged. The oval green fruits have a floral, tropical flavour.

The fruit of apple guavas commonly has green skin and pink flesh and a sweet flavour almost like nectar. This tree has large, light green leaves with prominent veins giving them a slightly pleated look.

The strawberry or cherry guava has small, shiny leaves and small, juicy fruit that some say has the best flavour of all.

🏃 HARVESTING

The best-flavoured apple guavas are tree-ripened – their skin should have yellowed and should give slightly under pressure, and the fruit should be fragrant.

However, guavas do continue to ripen off

the tree so you can also pick them green – and if you're making jam they contain more pectin when slightly underripe.

Strawberry or cherry guavas are a deep rose colour when ripe. Feijoas are best left to drop from the tree, as this is when they are fully ripe. Simply pick them up from the ground soon after they've dropped.

STORING

While apple guavas and strawberry or cherry guavas have edible skin, the feijoa's skin is inedible – the best way to eat a feijoa is to cut it in half and scoop out the flesh with a teaspoon.

Feijoa and strawberry or cherry guavas should be stored in the refrigerator and eaten within a few days. Apple guavas picked while still green should keep at room temperature for around 5 days. When ripe, they will keep another few days stored in a perforated plastic bag in the crisper.

Apple and strawberry or cherry guavas make great smoothies, blended up skin and all. Both varieties can also be frozen whole in bags for up to 6 months and defrosted later for making jam – just sit them in a colander and allow them to return to room temperature.

All guavas including feijoas can also be frozen in a syrup made with 1 part sugar to 2 parts water. Cut apple guavas into quarters and strawberry or cherry guavas in half, or scoop out feijoa flesh, and cover in the syrup. (This can later be made into sorbet.) Each fruit can also be frozen as an unsweetened purée. Fruit frozen either way should keep for up to 12 months.

Making guava fruit leather is another idea – for directions see Mangoes, page 38.

See recipe on page 186

MANGOES

☀ GROWING

Although mangoes prefer a tropical climate, they will happily thrive in the subtropics and even more temperate zones if protected from frost when young. The variety nam doc mai is reasonably tolerant of cold.

Mangoes grow into large trees up to 35 m (115 ft) tall, although the royal red variety is a moderate-sized plant for backyards. Plant your tree in an open sunny position protected from winds. Ensure the soil is well drained, has lots of organic matter, and is mulched. Grafted trees will bear sooner, fruiting in 3–4 years and producing well 10 years from planting. Apply lime in winter where soils are acidic, and watch out for fruit bats, fruit fly, scale insects, black spot and anthracnose, a fungus that causes black dots on the leaves and can also spread to the fruit (treatments include copper spray and applying potash in winter).

🦘 HARVESTING

Mangoes will continue to ripen indoors but are sweetest if allowed to ripen on the tree, so wait until your mangoes have coloured before picking. Pick the fruit with a 5 cm (2 in) stem so the sap doesn't burn the skin of the mango. Many people use a 'picking stick' to reach higher fruits. If you want green mangoes, just pick them once they have reached full size but have yet to change colour.

☰ STORING

Mangoes can get damaged in the cold of the refrigerator so are best stored at room temperature until completely ripe (and then refrigerated for another few days if necessary – but don't put them in a bag as they like airflow). They should last about a week in the fruit bowl (although they always seem to be eaten by then at my place!).

Mango can be frozen for use in smoothies and sorbets. **To freeze mango**, peel and slice the mangoes and lay the slices over a tray covered with baking paper, and freeze. Once frozen, pack into zip-lock bags removing as much air as possible. Alternatively, purée mango and freeze in airtight containers. Mango can be kept frozen for up to 12 months.

To dry mango, peel slightly underripe mangoes and cut into very thin slices with a vegetable peeler. Put them on a lightly oiled

wire rack set on a tray in an oven heated to its lowest temperature, with the fan on and the door slightly ajar. Dry them for 30 minutes, then turn them over and dry for another 30 minutes, or until the slices are dry but tacky to touch. Leave to cool in the oven, then store in a jar in the refrigerator for up to 12 months – but check after a week to make sure there is no condensation. If there is, dry the mango in the oven a little longer. If preferred, dried mango can be stored in the freezer for up to 2 years.

You can also dry mango slices in the sun – place the fruit on a rack on a table and cover with muslin (cheesecloth) so that bugs and dirt don't land on the fruit. Place the legs of the table in saucers of water to stop insects crawling up from the ground. The fruit should be left out in hot sunshine for 5–7 days, but brought in at night.

You can also dry green mango. This is traditionally ground (you can use a coffee grinder) to make *amchoor* ('*am*' is mango and '*choor*' is powder in Hindi), which is used like a spice in curries, adding a sour flavour.

To make mango fruit leather, purée the flesh and spread it thinly on a tray lined with baking paper. It can be sprinkled with a little sugar or even some salt flakes, or left au naturel, before being dried in an oven heated to its lowest temperature with the fan on and with the door slightly ajar. Dry for 3–4 hours. Check after 2 hours, and regularly from then until it is dry to touch but still pliable. Allow to cool, then cut into strips while still on the baking paper. Store in a tight-fitting airtight container in a cool, dark place for up to 1 month, or in the freezer for up to 12 months.

See recipes on pages 184, 234, 244 and 321

OLIVES

☀ GROWING

The silvery grey foliage of olive trees makes them a delightful feature in the garden, or an amazing screen that can provide fruit and oil for the kitchen. Of course the fruit must be cured, as fresh olives are unpalatable.

Olive trees are versatile – growing happily in pots, as espaliers, or freestanding in the garden – and are also hardy to drought and frost and can cope with salt-laden winds. Indeed, the trees often look their most character-filled the more elements they have endured.

The things olive trees don't cope with are high humidity and poor drainage, and they do need regular water in late winter and spring when they are flowering and starting to form fruit. A complete plant food once a year will also help trees grow well and crop reliably.

Olives take around 5 years to fruit well, but will then continue to produce for over a century. In fact, the world's oldest olive tree can be found in Crete and is thought to be between 3000 and 5000 years old!

🦅 HARVESTING

Fruit appears from late summer onwards, starting green and turning reddish-purple and eventually black as they ripen. Wait until the fruit is full-sized, then harvest when it is the colour and flavour you prefer. Green olives taste sharper and have a crisper texture, while black olives are fruitier and softer and have a higher oil content. If desired you can harvest olives at both stages – an early picking of green olives, followed by picking the remainder later when black.

The best method of harvesting is to cover the ground under the tree with a sheet, shade cloth or hessian and use long-handled vibrating tongs or a comb (which actually looks more like a plastic-tined rake) to remove the fruits, allowing them to drop to the material below.

▤ STORING

Fresh olives can be stored in a plastic bag in the refrigerator for up to 2 weeks before curing. There are different curing methods, including brining or dry-curing with salt. To brine olives, see the recipe on page 329.

To dry-cure black olives, place the olives in a plastic colander generously layered with rock salt, ensuring each olive is in contact with the salt. Place the colander inside a bowl and leave at room temperature for 1 week. The olives will wrinkle as they cure. Taste at the end of the week – if still bitter, continue curing and tasting daily until the desired flavour is reached. Rinse off the salt and transfer to sterilised jars. Cover in olive oil or a weak brine made up of 110 g (4 oz) of salt to every 1 litre (34 fl oz/4 cups) of water, and store in a cool, dark place for up to 12 months.

See recipe on page 329

PAPAYAS

☀ GROWING

Sometimes called paw paws, papayas are a soft-wooded perennial from the tropics that grow to about 4 m (13 ft) tall. In addition to the common orange-fleshed papaya, there are varieties with golden and pink or red flesh. They like deep soils with high organic matter, and good drainage is very important to prevent root rot. Papayas are either male, female or bisexual. The sex of the plant can't be determined until it starts to flower, unless you buy a grafted specimen with the sex already known and labelled.

The plants should be mulched with straw and kept weed free and protected from frost. Growing them against a brick wall is often enough to create a warm microclimate if you live outside the tropics or subtropics. You can prune out the centre of the tree if they are growing too tall. Papayas produce fruit when relatively young, just 10–16 months from planting, and trees yield about 12 kg (26½ lb) of fruit per plant each year.

🦅 HARVESTING

If you are picking fruit for green papaya salad, you can pick it as soon as it is full size. However to eat papaya fresh at its most fragrant and sweet, you should pick it when the skin has started to yellow. Cut them from the plant with a short stem attached and place them in a padded or polystyrene box to minimise bruising, as ripe papaya is a fragile fruit that is easily damaged.

☰ STORING

Papayas that have coloured but are not fully ripe will keep at room temperature for 2–5 days. Once ripe, place them in a plastic bag and keep refrigerated for up to 1 week. You can also freeze papaya – peel, seed and cut up the fruit and place on a tray lined with baking paper. Freeze for 4 hours, then pack into zip-lock bags removing as much air as possible and store in the freezer for up to 12 months. Use frozen papaya for smoothies and sorbets.

See recipe on page 235

PASSIONFRUIT

☀ GROWING

Passionfruit need a frost-free position, and north-east or north-west facing is ideal – the sunnier the better. They are a climbing plant and need a support of some kind for the tendrils to cling to. Lattice or chain wire measuring 3 x 3 m (10 x 10 ft) is ideal.

The plant likes well-drained soil with added organic matter and lots of regular fertiliser and water. Passionfruit can begin to fruit just 6 months after planting, but tend to crop well for just 4 years. During this time, however, they can produce 30 kg (66 lb) of fruit per year. When the plant starts to decline, it is simply time to plant another passionfruit vine.

Buying a grafted plant is recommended, partly because they are less prone to viral and bacterial problems. Nellie kelly is a purple passionfruit that is popular in cooler areas, while panama red and panama gold are larger-fruited types that are also great to eat, and which prefer a warm climate. You will need bees to pollinate your vine, so be careful not to spray when they are foraging. Wet weather during flowering unfortunately reduces crop set.

🦘 HARVESTING

Passionfruit will drop off the vine when they are fully coloured and ripe, but can also be snipped off with secateurs.

≡ STORING

Passionfruit can be stored at room temperature for 2 weeks, or in the refrigerator for 1 month. The skin of purple varieties will slightly wrinkle as they continue to ripen, but should be eaten before they heavily wrinkle as this means they are overripe.

The fruits can also be frozen whole in bags, or with the pulp scooped into ice-cube trays then transferred into zip-lock bags, for up to 6 months.

See recipes on pages 162, 286 and 335

PEACHES AND NECTARINES

 GROWING

Peaches and their smooth-skinned cousins, nectarines, are among the prettiest of backyard fruit trees. They have either pink or white or bicoloured blossoms in spring, and older trees often have gently weeping branches. They love a well-drained, slightly acidic soil in a sheltered and sunny position. If the winds are cold or the area is prone to late frosts, they can still be grown against a sunny wall.

The self-fertile trees should start to bear after only a few years, with nectarines always producing slightly smaller crops than peaches. They will give substantial crops after 4 years, and from this time you may have to start removing some fruit when they reach the size of a pea, giving 15 cm (6 in) gaps between fruit so that the tree has enough energy to grow its fruit well. The trees continue producing for at least 15 years, but need to be pruned each winter to encourage new shoots, as it is these that bear flowers and fruit. Use a copper spray to prevent leaf curl, applying when the tree is in bloom and the leaf buds are just about to open, and watch for aphids on new growth, which can usually be controlled with a soap spray. Also keep your crop netted to protect from birds.

You can choose between white-fleshed and yellow-fleshed varieties, and there are also clingstone peaches. Varieties that have low chilling requirements are the best for warmer areas. Goldmine is a popular white-fleshed nectarine that bears mid-season.

 HARVESTING

Peaches and nectarines will continue to ripen after they have been picked. Look at the suture line to see if it has started to soften and colour as an indicator of when to pick. Pick the fruit with a gentle twist and lift.

STORING

Pack peaches or nectarines stem-end down in a box lined with paper, with the fruit no more than 2 layers deep. They should keep this way in a cool place for 1–2 weeks.

To freeze peaches or nectarines, blanch them in boiling water for 30 seconds then

refresh them in iced water. This brief cooking prevents their skins from toughening in the freezer (you can also peel them if preferred). Slice if desired and spread them out on a tray lined with baking paper. Freeze until hard, then pack into zip-lock bags removing as much air as possible. Other alternatives are to purée the fruit or immerse them in a syrup made with 1 part sugar to 2 parts water and freeze in airtight containers. Peaches and nectarines can be frozen for up to 12 months.

To dry peaches or nectarines, prepare a bowl of water with a few vitamin C tablets (ascorbic acid) added. Halve and stone the fruit and soak in the water for 10 minutes, which prevents browning. Lay the fruit skin-side down on a wire rack set on a tray and place in an oven heated to its lowest temperature, with the fan on and the door slightly ajar. Dry for about 8 hours before turning, then continue drying until the fruit is leathery though still pliable. Leave to cool in the oven.

In hot weather peaches and nectarines can be dried on a table in the sun, but care needs to be taken that the fruit is covered with muslin (cheesecloth) so that bugs and dirt don't land on the fruit. Placing the legs of the table in saucers of water can stop insects from crawling up from the ground. The fruit should be left out in hot sunshine for 3–4 days, but brought in at night.

Store the dried fruit in a jar, but check after a week to make sure there is no condensation. If there is, dry the fruit a little longer. It should keep for up to 6 months in a cool, dark place; 12 months in the refrigerator; or 2 years in the freezer.

See recipes on pages 248, 306 and 335

PEARS

☀ GROWING

Pears are handsome trees growing to about 5 m (16 ft) tall. They have dark green foliage, elegant grey branching in winter when they are bare, and white spring blossoms. They crop from late summer into autumn and normally start to bear 2–3 years after planting, cropping well 4–7 years down the track, and often continuing to bear for at least half a century.

Pears normally need another variety planted nearby in order to bear fruit, though the williams pear, otherwise known as the bartlett, is partially self-fertile. They like a temperate to cool temperate climate and are tolerant of a wide range of soils. The trees develop a deep root system, which enjoys a good soak in dry periods. Feed pear trees with complete plant food in spring and watch out for codling moth, a problem that pears share with apples (for more information see page 19), and also watch for the pear and cherry slug. This is actually a leaf-eating caterpillar that can be organically controlled by grazing chickens around the base of the tree in winter (to eat the pupae), using glue barriers around the trunk, and even dusting the leaves with ash.

🐦 HARVESTING

Pears can easily be left too long on the tree as the flesh ripens from the inside out, meaning that by the time they are soft to touch on the branch they are probably brown and mealy on the inside. The fruit and its stem should easily come away from the tree with a simple upward twist; however, beurre bosc pears may need to be clipped off the tree.

≡ STORING

Fresh, firm pears keep well in perforated plastic bags in the crisper, and can last 2–4 months this way. When you want to eat them, just bring them out of the refrigerator and let them ripen and soften for a few days.

To dry pears, the williams (bartlett) pear is the best variety. Prepare a bowl of water with a few vitamin C tablets (ascorbic acid) added. Halve and core the pears and cut into eighths, then soak them in the water for 10 minutes, which prevents them from browning. Drain, then lay them skin-side down on a wire rack set on a tray and place in an oven preheated to its lowest temperature, with the fan on and the door slightly ajar. Dry for about 14 hours, or until the flesh is dry and feels like suede. Leave to cool in the oven. Store the dried pears in a jar, but check after a week to make sure there is no condensation. If there is, dry the pears in the oven a little longer. They should keep for up to 6 months in a cool, dark place; 12 months in the refrigerator; or 2 years in the freezer.

See recipes on pages 308 and 340

PINEAPPLES

 GROWING

Pineapples come from a warm-climate plant that produces its fruit as a spike above a bromeliad-like clump. Its silvery grey leaves are striking, and it does well as a pot plant as well as in the ground, where it needs good drainage, slightly acidic soil and a frost-free position. To grow pineapples in colder areas, you need a glasshouse or sunroom to overwinter them.

Pineapple plants grow to about 1 m (3 ft 4 in) tall and take around 2 years to fruit. While each plant only produces a single fruit before dying, they produce side 'pups' regularly, and these can be removed for growing new plants. The best fertiliser for pineapples is orchid and bromeliad food.

 HARVESTING

Pineapples continue to ripen after they are picked but are sweetest if allowed to ripen on the bush. The base of the pineapple will ripen and yellow first. Wait until the fruit is two-thirds yellow before picking it. Bend the stalk and cut just below the fruit with a knife, making sure you wear long sleeves to protect your arms as the leaves are sharp.

☰ STORING

Store pineapples at room temperature for a few days or in the refrigerator in a perforated plastic bag for up to 1 week.

To freeze pineapple, peel and core it, cut it up and pack into an airtight container, or cover with a syrup made with 1 part sugar to 2 parts water. Store in the freezer for up to 12 months.

To dry pineapple, peel and core it and chop into 2 cm (¾ in) chunks. Place on a tray lined with baking paper and put in an oven heated to its lowest temperature, with the fan on and the door slightly ajar. Dry for about 12 hours, turning the pieces halfway through. The pineapple should be chewy and sticky when ready. Leave to cool in the oven. Store the pineapple in a jar, but check after a week to make sure there is no condensation. If there is, dry the pineapple in the oven a little longer. It should keep in a cool, dark place for up to 6 months; in the refrigerator for up to 12 months; or in the freezer for up to 2 years.

See recipes on pages 164, 176, 232, 259 and 286

PLUMS

 ## GROWING

Plums can be a great tree for the backyard. Growing to about 4 x 4 m (13 x 13 ft), they tolerate a wide range of soils, and some varieties such as damsons, santa rosa and d'agen are either partially or entirely self-fertile, meaning you only need one tree for fruit. Some newer fruiting varieties even have that beautiful copper-coloured foliage that used to be the domain of ornamental types.

Plums are divided into European and Japanese varieties. European plum trees are slightly smaller, and so is the fruit. They include most of the yellow-fleshed plums such as sugar and angelina and prefer slightly cooler climates. Japanese plums include santa rosa and mariposa.

Importantly, plums can bear very well if the season has suited them. So laden can their branches be that they can easily break under the burden, so thinning them to prevent over-cropping is prudent. They respond well to a deep soaking in dry weather and complete plant food in spring. Watch out for pear and cherry slug (see Pears, page 49), which can also damage plum tree leaves. Net plum trees to keep the fruit safe from birds.

 ## HARVESTING

Plums should be picked with a small stem intact. For cooking and preserving, they are best picked slightly before they are ripe, whereas for eating or freezing, they should be picked when fully sweet and soft to touch, especially near the base. Colour is not a good indication as it varies depending on type.

STORING

Ripe plums can be stored in a perforated plastic bag in the crisper for up to 2 weeks. If you would like to store your plums longer, say for up to 4 weeks, pick them slightly underripe. When you are ready to eat them, bring them back to room temperature and put them in a paper bag to increase the gas around the fruit that triggers ripening.

To freeze plums, blanch them in boiling water for 30 seconds then refresh them in iced water. This brief cooking prevents their skins from toughening in the freezer. Spread on a tray lined with baking paper and freeze until hard, then pack into zip-lock bags removing as much air as possible. Alternatively, purée the plums and store in airtight containers (you could use this at a later date to make plum sauce). Plums can be frozen for up to 12 months.

Plums can also be sun-dried or oven-dried in the same way as apricots (see page 21). The d'agen plum is ideal for this as it is the prune plum.

See recipes on pages 224, 264 and 337

RASPBERRIES AND BLACKBERRIES

 ## GROWING

The bramble berries botanically known as *Rubus* include raspberries and blackberries, and also boysenberries, loganberries and youngberries. They like full sun with shelter from hot westerly winds, and also require some structure or framework to grow on, be it a wire fence or a structure called a cradle that can be bought specially for the purpose. The plants have thorns, so care needs to be taken when you are picking or pruning.

The fruit of most varieties appears after flowering in summer, and often a second flush happens in autumn. Berries are particularly delicious to birds as well as people so will need netting at this time. The plants do best in free-draining, slightly acidic soil that is enriched with organic matter annually, and require a cold chill over winter to give them a proper dormancy to produce fruits in any number. You can expect up to about 5 kg (11 lb) of fruit per plant each year if grown well. Summer-fruiting varieties need to have the older canes removed at the end of the season, making way for newer canes to fruit the following summer.

 ## HARVESTING

Berries are sweetest when they have reached their deepest colour, and are best picked first thing in the morning. Raspberries need to be gently pulled from their core and stem with your fingers, which leaves the centre of the berry hollow. Blackberries retain their core.

Always use shallow baskets when picking, and don't pile the berries more than about 3 deep to avoid bruising them.

STORING

Fully ripe berries are best enjoyed the day you pick them, but can be stored in the refrigerator for 2–3 days.

To freeze berries, spread them across a tray lined with baking paper. Once frozen, transfer them into zip-lock bags removing as much air as possible and store in the freezer for up to 12 months.

Berries make beautiful jams, sauces, cordials and even vinegar (see Raspberry vinegar, page 218).

See recipes on pages 167, 174, 218, 266 and 334

ROCKMELONS

 GROWING

Melons are scrambling plants that will cover the ground or, if trained, can grow up a trellis. They are annuals, love a frost-free position (they are normally planted in spring from seed), and require regular feeding and water to do well. They are dioecious too, meaning they produce male and female flowers, so it's important to encourage bees to pollinate the flowers to produce fruits. If this is impossible (for example, in a glasshouse) or if pollination just doesn't seem to be happening, then you can use a paintbrush to spread the pollen from flower to flower. Also, if you are growing melons on a trellis, then the fruit will need to be bagged in a net to support them like a sling, as they can weigh 1–3 kg (2 lb 3 oz–6 lb 10 oz) depending on the variety.

Some melons have netted skin, others smooth; some have almost salmon-coloured flesh and others yellow, green or even white. Honeydew melons are a member of the same species. Soon after fruit has set, you should pinch off the growing stem and begin feeding the plant with a high-potash fertiliser. This will encourage side shoots and additional fruit to form, and ensure that the fruit has good flavour. Lift the fruit off the ground onto an upturned plastic pot, or place fresh straw underneath so that you protect the fruit from rot. Each plant should give 4 melons.

HARVESTING

Melons have a wonderful aroma when fully ripe. They soften at their outer end and should easily pull from the vine, but benefit from another day or two inside developing to their best.

☰ STORING

Once ripe, whole melons can be stored in the refrigerator for up to 1 week, and cut pieces will keep for 3 days covered with plastic wrap.

For something different, make a sugar syrup with 1 part sugar to 2 parts water and add some fragrant spices such as star anise, cinnamon and cloves. Peel the melon into ribbons and toss it through the cooled syrup. This sweetened, spiced melon is delicious and keeps in the refrigerator for 1 week, and can also be frozen for up to 12 months (it can even be made into sorbet later).

See recipe on page 180

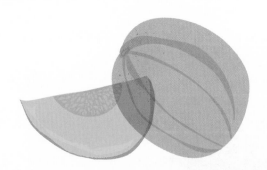

STRAWBERRIES

☀ GROWING

Strawberries are a low ground-covering plant with dark green trifoliate leaves, which means that 3 leaflets are attached to each stem like a clover. They can be grown from the tropics to the mountains as there are many varieties. There are also many ways of growing them, such as in a patch or 'matted rows' as they are known, where all the runners are allowed to thread the plants in the row together. Other ways include strawberry pots with spouted sides, regular pots, hanging baskets, bags or even barrels with 5 cm (2 in) holes drilled into the sides for the strawberries to grow out of.

The plants need sun and most of all, a rich and well-drained soil with lots of organic matter. They also need netting from birds, and often straw (or plastic) is used around the plant to stop fruit from touching the ground and rotting. Any damaged berries, whether from sunburn, insect injury or other causes, should be removed from the plant as rot can spread to other berries. New plants can be grown from runners (or stolons), but unless growing strawberries in a matted row you should remove these as they limit the amount of fruit the main plant produces.

HARVESTING

Berries to be eaten immediately may be picked at any time, but if you plan to keep them longer, pick them in the early morning or on cool, cloudy days, as warm berries are soft and bruise easily. Pinch the stem with your fingertip and thumb, trying not to handle the berries themselves. Gently place the berries into your bucket, and never overfill it as the berries at the bottom will get crushed. Keep the berries in the shade until you can put them in the refrigerator.

☰ STORING

Strawberries keep a few days in the refrigerator, but really are best within half a day of picking.

To freeze strawberries, spread hulled fruit across a tray lined with baking paper. Once frozen, transfer into zip-lock bags removing as much air as possible and store in the freezer for up to 12 months. Another idea is to stir whole or chopped strawberries through softened vanilla ice-cream, refreeze it and eat within 3 months.

To make strawberry syrup, combine an equal weight of caster (superfine) sugar and strawberries (hulled and chopped or left whole) in a saucepan. Add a splash of water and some vanilla bean, split and scraped. Bring to the boil, stirring until the sugar dissolves, then simmer for 30 minutes. Ladle into warm sterilised jars. Store in a cool, dark place for up to 12 months. This is perfect on pancakes.

See recipes on pages 266, 271 and 334

WATERMELONS

☀ GROWING

Plant watermelons from seed as soon as the cold weather has finished. The vines need lots of sunshine, water and plenty of organic matter to grow to their best. For really successful vines, create a small mound of well-dug earth mixed with 50 per cent well-rotted manure. Plant 3–4 seeds half a thumb deep, and thin to the 2 strongest seedlings once they have emerged. Like all members of the cucurbit family, there are male and female flowers on the same vine. This means you may need to hand-pollinate by spreading pollen from flower to flower with a paintbrush if you have poor weather or not enough bees in your area. Each plant usually produces just 2 melons, but as individual fruit can easily grow up to 14 kg (31 lb), the plants should be fed regularly with liquid fertiliser or pelletised manure to ensure the fruit has good flavour. Soon after the fruit sets, you should pinch off the growing stems. It takes around 16 weeks from seed to harvest.

Watermelons come in many types – aside from the common red some have golden flesh and others orange or white. Check out heirloom seed suppliers for the most interesting varieties.

🕊 HARVESTING

It is best to determine the ripeness of a watermelon by sound. Those that make a hollow sound when tapped are usually ready, but you can double-check this by looking at the spot where the melon is in contact with the ground – it should be yellow.

☰ STORING

Watermelons will keep in a cool, dark place for 4 days, but will last longer in the refrigerator. Once cut, cover with plastic wrap and keep refrigerated for a week or so.

Watermelon does not freeze well unless made into sorbet. **To make watermelon sorbet**, make a syrup with 230 g (8 oz/1 cup) of caster (superfine) sugar and 500 ml (17 fl oz/ 2 cups) of water. Purée 1.2 kg (2 lb 10 oz) of watermelon flesh, then blend in the cooled syrup (work in batches if necessary). Pour into a wide metal tray and freeze until almost set. Use a food processor to blend the sorbet to a smooth texture, then refreeze it in an airtight container, where it can be stored for up to 6 months. Before serving, whip 1 egg white to stiff peaks in a food processor. Add half the watermelon mixture in pieces and blend together. Refreeze for another 4–5 hours. You can blend the remaining watermelon mixture with another egg white to serve at a later date.

See recipe on page 301

VEGETABLE PATCH

ARTICHOKES, GLOBE

☀ GROWING

The globe artichoke is a very pretty addition to the garden. Its thistle-like flowers and silvery grey, deeply serrated leaves make a bold statement and work equally well planted in the flower garden as in the vegetable patch. Growing to around 1.5 m (5 ft) tall, it is native to North Africa and loves warm climates (though not overly humid ones). It likes soil with lots of added organic matter, an annual dressing of lime, and good drainage. Mulching well helps reduce water loss in summer and protect from very cold winters, too. Feed with liquid fertiliser every few months. Cut the foliage back to about 10 cm (4 in) off the ground in winter and it will burst with new growth in spring. The plants produce their flower heads in spring and summer, with another flush in autumn if you're lucky, and 2–3 plants provide a good amount of artichokes for a family.

After about 4 years the plants start to be past their best, and new off-shoots from the side of the clump should be taken in spring or autumn as replacements. Make sure each piece has a good section of root and trim back the leaves before planting. Water with seaweed solution to help them cope with the transplant shock. Nip off the new plant's flower buds the first year so the plant can become sturdier, and only allow a few flower buds to form the second year.

🕊 HARVESTING

Beautiful as artichoke flowers are, the trick is not to let them open! Pick them when they are compact and green, about the size of a tennis ball. Cut them off with about 15 cm (6 in) of stem attached. Afterwards, trim back the stem that remains on the plant to half its height, which will encourage new shoots.

≡ STORING

Artichokes are best used fresh, but can be kept for a week in the crisper. Don't wash them before refrigerating, but sprinkle with a little water before putting them in a plastic bag.

To prepare artichokes for cooking, get a bowl of water ready with lemon juice added. Working with 1 artichoke at a time, remove about half of its leaves. Cut off the top third of the artichoke and discard, and trim the stem to about 5–7 cm (2–2¾ in) long. Cut the artichoke in half lengthways and scoop out the hairy choke. Rub a cut lemon over all the exposed surfaces of the artichoke, then drop the pieces into the lemon water (the lemon prevents browning) until ready to cook.

To freeze artichokes, cook artichoke halves in boiling water for 15–20 minutes. Drain well and sprinkle with a little lemon juice. Freeze in airtight containers for up to 12 months.

See recipe on page 324

ASPARAGUS

☀ GROWING

Asparagus is a perennial vegetable, so planting it with care initially will reward you in the long term. After the production of spears in spring, the plant grows to around 1.5 m (5 ft) tall with feathery fronds that make quite a pretty foliage contrast in the garden.

The easiest way to plant asparagus is by purchasing crowns, which are clumps of roots from which new plants can grow, in winter or early spring. These need to be planted in a hole that easily accommodates the crown, about 20 cm (8 in) deep, and mounded slightly over the top. The soil needs to be free-draining and well dug with manure and compost, and with a pH of around 6.5, which is slightly acidic. Keep the area weed free and well watered, and cut your plants back to the ground each year and mulch with straw. Remove any berries that appear in summer and most importantly, keep your patience for at least a few years before you start harvesting your spears.

🌿 HARVESTING

The amount of asparagus you are able to cut depends on the age and vigour of the clump. Normally none is harvested for the first 3 years, and only a few weeks of trimming in the fourth year is recommended. The good news is that, for the next 15–20 years, you can pick asparagus each spring for a few months.

Use a serrated knife to cut below the surface when the spear is 10–20 cm (4–8 in) tall.

≡ STORING

Asparagus can be kept like a bunch of flowers, tied together with a rubber band if necessary, with the fresh-cut stems placed in a glass with about 4 cm (1½ in) of clean water. They can be kept for a few weeks in the refrigerator this way (a good spot is in the door). Alternatively, wrap the bunch in a damp tea towel and place in a plastic bag for storing in the crisper. To prepare asparagus, you need to cut off the woody bases and remove any hard scales on the sides of the spears, which is easily done with a vegetable peeler.

To freeze asparagus, blanch spears for 1–2 minutes depending on their thickness, before cooling in iced water. Drain and spread on a clean tea towel to dry, then pack into zip-lock bags removing as much air as possible. Asparagus can be stored in the freezer for up to 12 months and can be used direct from the freezer without defrosting.

Asparagus can also be dried. **To dry asparagus**, boil spears for 2–4 minutes depending on their thickness, then drain and spread on a clean tea towel to dry. Next, preheat your oven to its lowest temperature with the fan on and spread the spears across wire racks set on trays. Place the trays in the oven and leave the door slightly ajar to let the steam escape. Check the spears after 2 hours, making sure they are not scorching. Turn off the heat when the spears are nearly dry and are leathery to touch (normally after about 6 hours). Leave in the oven for another hour

to cool. Store in jars, but check after a week to make sure there is no condensation. If there is, dry the asparagus in the oven a little longer. Store in a cool, dark place for up to 6 months. To use, just soak the dried spears in cold water for 30 minutes, then bring to the boil and immediately remove from the heat. The asparagus can be served as it is or chopped and added to different dishes.

To pickle asparagus and store in oil, cut the spears into 2 or 3 lengths. Put them in a large saucepan and cover with equal parts water and white vinegar and bring to the boil. Cook for 3–4 minutes. Drain and spread on a clean tea towel to dry. Half-fill sterilised jars with olive or vegetable oil. Add the asparagus and some garlic, mint or chilli before covering with more oil. The asparagus will keep for just over a week, but longer if stored in the refrigerator or if you heat-process the jars (see page 12). The asparagus is a real treat to have on hand for adding to antipasto plates or salads.

See recipe on page 325

BEANS

☀ GROWING

Beans come in many varieties, from dwarf or bush beans to climbing beans that trail up a tripod or trellis. While most beans are summer annuals, there are also climbing perennial beans called runner beans that produce flat beans, and which die down each winter to an underground rootstock but re-emerge in spring.

Annual varieties need to be sown after the frosts have finished. Many people like to plant their beans in a mound, which helps the soil warm up and also aids with drainage. Beans can also be grown in tubs. They love regular water, and you should be munching away in 10 weeks.

The plants produce more and more beans the more you pick, so harvest them continually every 4 days or so to keep the plants productive. They also produce their own nitrogen in special nodules on their roots, which helps them grow. The nitrogen also benefits crops to follow, so dig the entire plant back into the ground when the crop has finished and you'll be feeding up your soil too.

If growing the climbing variety, your tripod or trellis should be about 1.8 m (6 ft) tall. Climbers include blue lake, purple king and rattlesnake. They yield around 1 kg (2 lb 3 oz) per plant, as do runner beans.

Runner beans will survive around 7 years. Varieties include scarlet runner, which has beautiful red blooms, and painted lady, which has bicoloured flowers in salmon and white.

Dwarf beans include purple queen, dragon's tongue, which has lemon and purple streaked pods, and a lovely golden bean from yesteryear called sex without strings. Dwarf beans don't produce as many beans but are much faster to bear and can be repeat-planted in the one season.

Broad beans are from a different genus and so have a different growing habit. They are planted in late autumn and winter, providing their beans in spring.

HARVESTING

When picking fresh beans, be careful not to damage the plant by pulling off the beans – cut or snip them off instead.

For dried beans, simply leave the beans to mature on the plant until the leaves have withered, then hang the plants undercover to dry before podding. Leave the beans to air-dry for a few days before putting into jars, where they will store in a cool, dark place for many years.

All varieties can be dried, and this is also the way to save seeds for next year's planting. However, borlotti beans, red kidney beans and flageolet beans are some of the classic drying varieties, with others including cherokee wax, which has black beans inside yellow pods, and frost, a bicoloured black and white bean.

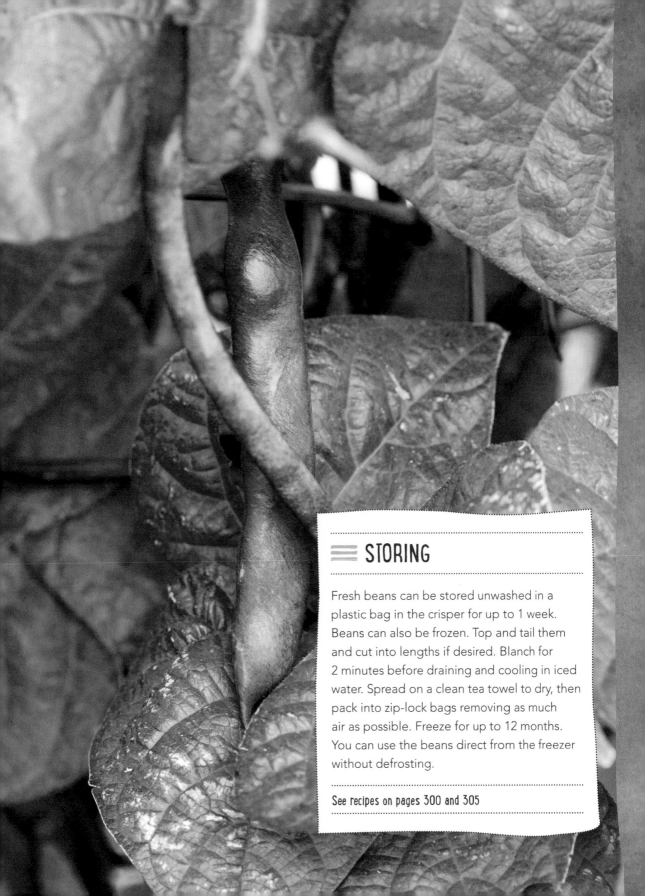

STORING

Fresh beans can be stored unwashed in a plastic bag in the crisper for up to 1 week. Beans can also be frozen. Top and tail them and cut into lengths if desired. Blanch for 2 minutes before draining and cooling in iced water. Spread on a clean tea towel to dry, then pack into zip-lock bags removing as much air as possible. Freeze for up to 12 months. You can use the beans direct from the freezer without defrosting.

See recipes on pages 300 and 305

BEETROOT

GROWING

The earthy sweetness of beetroot (beets) makes them a favourite raw, pickled and baked, and cooked into stews, soups and dips. They come in round (globe) and oval (cylindrical) shapes, and as well as the usual crimson colour you can get them in white, yellow and orange, and even with pink target-like circles when cut crossways in the variety called chioggia.

The seeds of beetroot are called conglomerate seeds, which means they are in a cluster that sprouts several plants, often needing thinning (the excess plants can be transplanted). They like a light soil with a slightly acidic pH that is fertile (although they prefer manure to be spread a while before planting), and can be planted year round. The seeds should be sown direct, but germinate better if they are soaked in a cup of water for a few hours first. They love food and benefit from regular applications of complete plant food. The moisture needs to be kept up as sudden wet spells can result in the roots splitting, while sudden dry spells can result in them going to seed. Beetroot can be ready as early as 8 weeks from planting.

HARVESTING

Beetroot are ready to lift when they are about the size of tennis balls. (They can also be picked smaller if desired.) Loosen the soil underneath your beetroot with a garden fork, being careful not to pierce the roots. Remove the leaves by twisting the stems about 5 cm (2 in) above the beetroot (too close will cause bleeding). The leaves can be eaten as a silverbeet (swiss chard) substitute.

STORING

Store beetroot in wooden boxes completely covered in dampened peat or coconut fibre with their stems still attached. Leave in a cool, dark place, where they should keep for months. This storage method seems to keep beetroot even longer than storing it in a plastic bag in the crisper.

To freeze beetroot, boil whole until tender, then rub off the skins. Freeze either whole or in slices, in zip-lock bags with as much air removed as possible, for up to 12 months. To use the beetroot, thaw it in the refrigerator and either add dressing, boil it briefly or bake it in the oven.

To dry beetroot, cut them into thin circles or use a vegetable peeler to cut thin strips. Place on a tray lined with baking paper and put in an oven heated to its lowest temperature with the fan on and the door slightly ajar. Dry for about

8 hours until brittle and chip-like. Leave to cool in the oven. Store the dried beetroot in a jar for up to 12 months, but check after a week to make sure there is no condensation. If there is, dry the beetroot in the oven a little longer. To use the beetroot, rehydrate it in cold water for 30 minutes and add to soups and stews. It also makes great chips – rehydrate it, dip into a light sugar syrup and place in a moderate oven until crisp.

See recipes on pages 254 and 293

BROCCOLI

GROWING

Broccoli likes a manure-enriched soil with some added lime blended in a few weeks before planting. The annual vegetable is valued for its repeat cropping – once the main head is cut off, smaller side shoots like broccolini are produced if it is kept well watered, and 1 kg (2 lb 3 oz) of harvest per plant is not unusual. Plant seeds in late summer after rain showers and they should develop over autumn and winter. Watch for cabbage moth and cover with muslin (cheesecloth) to exclude it if possible. You can also plant your broccoli near sage and strew with wormwood leaves or apply cooled wormwood tea to deter them. It is also worth checking the leaves regularly and removing caterpillars by hand.

 STORING

The trick to keeping broccoli is not to wash it until you are ready to use it – place it straight into a plastic bag and put it in the refrigerator, where it will keep for 5–7 days. Before cooking home-grown broccoli, it's a good idea to soak the heads in salted water for 30 minutes to help remove any hidden bugs.

To freeze broccoli, cut into florets and boil for 4 minutes before draining and plunging into iced water. Drain again and spread on a clean tea towel to dry. Pack into zip-lock bags removing as much air as possible and freeze for up to 12 months. You can use the broccoli direct from the freezer without defrosting.

See recipes on pages 200 and 300

HARVESTING

Pick broccoli early in the morning before the day warms up. The first head should be cut off with a short stem above a pair of leaves (use a serrated knife), which stimulates further shoots down the stem. Later in the season, watch that your heads don't break into flower when the weather gets hot.

CABBAGES AND KALE

GROWING

Like their close relatives in the brassica family – cauliflower and broccoli – cabbage and kale do best in soil with added lime, and they like ample water and cope with the winter cold remarkably well. In fact, frosts sweeten the flavour of both these vegetables. Cabbages take around 20 weeks from seed to harvest, but kale, which is an ancient type of cabbage, is much faster as it doesn't form a head. It should be ready for picking leaf by leaf after about 8 weeks. Kale can be highly ornamental with purple and frilly cultivars, and is more tolerant of heat and drought than cabbage. Plant cabbage and kale seeds in late summer, throughout autumn and into early winter. See Broccoli on page 73 for tips on controlling cabbage moth.

HARVESTING

Cabbage heads need to be firm and full to the touch and should not have started to split. Use a sharp knife to cut just below the head, leaving the lower leaves behind. You can leave the plant in the ground as sprouts will soon emerge where the head once was and these young leaves make delicious garden greens.

Kale grows in the 'cut and come again' style. New young leaves can be used in salads, while the older outside leaves will need cooking.

≡ STORING

Cabbages can be hung wrapped in paper inside a net bag, in a vermin- and frost-free shed or cellar for 3 months. They will also keep for weeks in a plastic bag in the crisper. Outside leaves may spoil with storage and need to be removed. Kale doesn't last so long after picking, so keep it in a plastic bag in the crisper and use it in a few days.

To freeze cabbage, shred it coarsely or cut into quarters. Blanch for 1–2 minutes (shredded) or 3 minutes (quarters) before cooling in iced water, draining and spreading on a clean tea towel to dry. Pack into zip-lock bags removing as much air as possible and freeze for up to 12 months.

To freeze kale, blanch young tender leaves for 1 minute, then cool in iced water. Drain and spread on a clean tea towel to dry. Chop the kale, pack it into zip-lock bags removing as much air as possible and freeze for up to 12 months.

To make sauerkraut, remove a few outer leaves of a medium cabbage until the leaves begin to turn pale. Finely shred the inner leaves and put in a large bowl. Sprinkle with 2 tablespoons of salt. Mix thoroughly with your hands, almost kneading it to help break the structure of the cabbage. Once the cabbage has become limp, start packing it into a sterilised crockpot as tightly as possible. You can add other ingredients to flavour the cabbage, such as crushed garlic or peppercorns.

Continue to pack the cabbage into the crock, pushing down with your fist so there are no air pockets. Pour on enough warm water to just cover the cabbage. Put a small plate on top of the cabbage and place something heavy on top to weight the cabbage down. Put the lid on the crock. Leave at room temperature for anywhere between 1 week and 6 months, depending on the sourness you prefer and also on the weather, as warm weather speeds up the fermenting process (I usually stop the fermenting at around 6 weeks). Remove any scum that forms on the surface. Transfer the finished sauerkraut to sterilised jars and store in the refrigerator for up to 6 months. Rinse before using.

See recipes on pages 199 and 294

CAPSICUMS AND CHILLIES

☀ GROWING

Capsicums (bell peppers) need plenty of warm weather to thrive and should not be planted out when temperatures are lower than 21°C (70°F), though plants can be raised earlier under cover. It takes about 16 weeks from seed until ripened fruit. Space plants about 60 cm (2 ft) apart, and make sure your soil has extra manure and compost. Plant in full sun and water regularly.

Capsicums range in colour and shape, from small bell types to longer horn-shaped types, and paprika is made from a Hungarian capsicum called alma paprika. Six plants of any type should feed the family as each plant normally yields over 1 kg (2 lb 3 oz). Heavily laden bushes might need staking, and you can use nets to protect them from bird attack and baits for fruit fly.

Chillies are a spicy form of capsicum tending to have smaller fruits. Many varieties are perennial, at least for a few seasons when in a frost-free location. They are prolific bearers, often with hundreds of chillies on each plant. Chillies are rated for their heat, but a general guide is the smaller the fruit, the hotter it is.

For mild heat, trying growing siam yellow. Jalapeños are one of the classic Mexican chillies, while chocolate habanero has deep brown, bell-shaped peppers with a sweet, fruity flavour to go with their incredible intensity. Zimbabwe bird's eye is another real heart-stopper for those who like it hot!

🗡 HARVESTING

Pick capsicums or chillies at whatever colour stage you prefer – the fruit has a sharpness when green that disappears and becomes sweeter and fruitier as it ripens. If picking green, wait until the fruit is full size and pick towards the time it begins to change colour. Snip off the fruits with a small stem attached.

☰ STORING

You can store capsicums and chillies in a plastic or paper bag in the crisper for 1 week.

To freeze capsicums, blanch them for 5 minutes, then put into a plastic bag to steam as they cool. Peel off their skins, cut them in half and remove the seeds. Pack into zip-lock bags removing as much air as possible and freeze for up to 12 months.

To dry capsicums, prepare them as for freezing then put them on a wire rack set over a tray. Place in an oven heated to its lowest temperature with the fan on and the door slightly ajar. Dry for about 12 hours, turning after about 5 hours, until brittle to touch. Leave to cool in the oven, then store in a jar in a cool, dark place for up to 12 months, but check after a week to make sure there is no condensation. If there is, dry the capsicum in the oven a little longer. To use, soak the capsicum in hot water.

To make paprika, just grind dried capsicum in a coffee grinder.

Chillies can be dried or smoked, but the fleshier the chilli, the more difficult this is. Fleshy chillies like habaneros are best frozen.

To freeze chillies, spread them on a tray lined with baking paper. When frozen, put into zip-lock bags removing as much air as possible and freeze for up to 12 months. Another method is to slice the chillies open, remove the seeds and chop the chillies (you could use a food processor), then freeze the chopped chilli in ice-cube trays. Once frozen, transfer the cubes to zip-lock bags.

To dry chillies, use thinner-fleshed chillies such as bird's eye or cayenne chillies, and choose mature specimens without any blemishes. Wash them in salty water to help combat mould. A string or ristra of chillies can be easily made with a needle and cotton thread, literally sewing through the chillies. Wear gloves to protect your hands while doing this. Put the string of chillies in a well-ventilated place out of direct sunlight.

An even easier way of drying chillies is just to hang whole plants upside down. Once the chillies are completely dry, store in jars in a cool, dark place for up to 12 months.

Of course you can also sun-dry chillies. Slice them in half and remove the seeds, and lay them cut-side down on trays lined with baking paper in the sunshine for about 3 days, bringing them in at night, until they are dry enough to break easily in your fingers.

Smoking red jalapeño chillies to make chipotle is an age-old Mexican technique. The flavour of the wet wood as it smokes permeates into the chilli and adds to its complexity. The type of wood you use also alters the flavour, with hickory, pear, apple and mesquite popular.

To smoke chillies, get hot coals burning well in a wood-fired barbecue with a lid, then add large water-soaked pieces of your chosen wood (I use apple or pear wood after pruning in the orchard, and soak the pieces in a bucket of water overnight). Put wire racks or baskets of de-stemmed, halved and seeded chillies (in a single layer) inside and put on the lid. It will take about 6 hours to smoke the chillies completely – they should be dry but still pliable. (For traditional chipotle you can leave the chillies whole, but the smoking may take longer.) The cooled chillies can be stored in jars in a cool, dark place for up to 12 months.

See recipes on pages 190, 192, 210, 216, 228, 230, 265, 319 and 328

CARROTS

 ## GROWING

Carrots have become a mainstay of many people's meals. But despite this the carrot is rarely explored to its full extent, with purple, white and yellow types remaining uncommon. Luckily for gardeners, many of these heirloom varieties are available as seed.

Carrots need a light and friable soil that is not overly rich in nutrients, as well as a sunny position. Remove all rocks and break up clods. Sow seed directly into the ground any time of year, although autumn is generally considered best, and press them in lightly without top-dressing as they don't like to be buried. Rows of carrots totalling 4–6 m (13–20 ft) in length are enough to feed a family, but you might like to make smaller plantings successively and spread your harvest.

Don't feed your carrots as this can cause the roots to fork instead of taper. The time from seed to plate is around 10–16 weeks, but you can normally pick baby carrots before this as you thin the rows. Watch for aphids, using a soap spray if necessary. Unusual carrot varieties to seek out include yellow lobbericher, purple dragon, which has almost red skin, and paris market, which has round roots.

HARVESTING

It's best to pull out your carrots when the soil is a little damp, as they slide out better this way – water the day before if necessary. Pull the carrots in one steady motion without twisting to avoid breaking off the tops. Carrots can hold in the ground for many months, giving you a long harvesting period – they just grow bigger!

STORING

If the refrigerator is full or your harvest huge, you can store carrots with their tops removed in a wooden box, packing them in layers with dampened peat, sand or coconut fibre in between. If you need to protect them from severe cold, you can insulate with straw around the boxes.

If there is space in the refrigerator, remove their leafy tops and store in a perforated plastic bag in the crisper for 2–3 weeks, or put them in an airtight container and cover with water, changing the water every 4–5 days – this way they should keep for a month or so.

To freeze carrots, peel and slice them and boil for 3 minutes. Drain, cool in iced water and drain again. Spread on a clean tea towel to dry, then pack into zip-lock bags removing as much air as possible and freeze for up to 12 months.

To dry carrots, prepare them as for freezing and spread over wire racks set over trays.

Dry them in an oven heated to its lowest temperature with the fan on and the door slightly ajar for about 6 hours, until they feel leathery and even a little crisp. Leave to cool in the oven. Store in jars in a cool, dark place for up to 12 months, but check after a week to make sure there is no condensation. If there is, dry the carrot in the oven a little longer. To use the dried carrot, soak it in cold water for about 1 hour before cooking.

See recipe on page 298

CAULIFLOWERS

· · · · · · · · · · · · · · · · ·

☀ GROWING

Cauliflower is best grown in cold weather, as the warmer it gets the more likely you will be bothered by cabbage moth, and also by your heads breaking into flower. Unlike broccoli it is not a repeat-harvesting plant, so the best way to ensure continuous cropping is to stagger planting. You can plant the first row in late summer (either directly from seed or from seedlings), and then every fortnight plant another, right up until late autumn. Cauliflowers like lime added to 'sweeten' the soil, and regular watering. Try heirloom types like purple of sicily and green macerata, which has a lime-coloured head. For ways of deterring cabbage moth, see Broccoli on page 73.

🕊 HARVESTING

Wait until the head is about 15 cm (6 in) across before harvesting, and be sure to cut it before the 'curd' breaks into flower. Use a sharp knife, cutting the head with about 5 cm (2 in) of stem.

≡ STORING

You can store cauliflower in a plastic bag in the crisper for up to 2 weeks. Cauliflower also freezes well. Cut it into florets and blanch in acidulated water (with 1 tablespoon of lemon juice or vinegar added, to prevent discolouring) for 3 minutes before draining and cooling in iced water. Drain again and spread on a clean tea towel to dry. Pack into zip-lock bags removing as much air as possible and store in the freezer for up to 12 months. You can use it direct from the freezer without defrosting.

See recipes on pages 250 and 300

CELERY

 GROWING

Celery likes consistency – regular food, water and weeding (it doesn't like competition). In terms of the soil, prepare your bed with lots of organic matter like compost or rotted animal manure, and dig the soil well and deep prior to planting. Celery uses a fair bit of calcium, so you can also sprinkle some lime on the soil.

Plant out seedlings about 20 cm (8 in) apart in autumn. Then be patient – celery takes about 5 months before it's ready to harvest. Frost will sweeten the taste of celery. A month before harvest, mound straw up around the plants or wrap them with cardboard or milk cartons to exclude the sun and turn the stems pale green. This is known as blanching. You can tie the stems together if necessary to stop them from blowing over.

 HARVESTING

Use a garden fork to lift the head of celery from underneath, then cut off the roots with a sharp knife. Stalks can also be picked from the plant one by one.

STORING

Trim the base of the celery and the tops of the leaves, wrap it in aluminium foil and store it in the crisper, where it will last for around 3 weeks. Celery can also be sliced, blanched and frozen, but this is only suitable for use in soups and casseroles as once defrosted the celery loses its form.

See recipe on page 255

CORN

☀ GROWING

Native to the Americas, corn is traditionally grown with climbing beans and pumpkin (winter squash) in what is known as the 'three sisters' method. The beans climb up the corn stalks while suppling nitrogen, and the pumpkins cover the ground as a living mulch.

Corn is a summer crop. To grow it, prepare your soil with lots of well-rotted manure, then soak the soil and plant seeds in pairs 1 cm (½ in) under the surface, 30 cm (1 ft) apart. Remove the least vigorous seedling after germination. (Alternatively, plant individual already established seedlings.) Mulch them and keep up the water, and feed with seaweed solution every 2 weeks so they grow quickly.

Corn should be planted in blocks to help with pollination, which is important for developing all the kernels on the cob. Overhead watering helps spread the pollen. Another option is to use a paintbrush to spread the pollen from the male flowers at the top of the stalk to the female flowers below.

You should get a few cobs per plant, and 16 plants will yield a good amount for a family, though they can be different varieties.

For example, white corn is super sweet and uncommon in shops, and the variety called honey and cream has a blend of white and yellow kernels on the cob.

with baking paper with some holes pierced through, or hanging in mesh bags. Store the corn in a jar in a cool, dark place, where it should last for many years.

 ## HARVESTING

Corn tells you it's ready to be picked when the silks at the top of each cob start to brown. Ripeness can also be double-checked by piercing through the husk to see what colour the kernels bleed – watery is unripe; milky is ripe. To pick, twist the cobs and push them down until they snap.

Leaving corn to mature on the plant is how you make popping corn. You can do this with any variety, although some are better suited and marketed that way. Once the husks are brown, rub off the kernels with your hands and dry them out for another 4–5 days in a warm, well-ventilated place, either on wire racks lined

STORING

To keep corn fresh for as long as possible, leave the husks on and store uncovered in the crisper, where it will keep for 4–5 days. Corn can also be frozen. Remove the husks from sweet young cobs and boil for about 5 minutes. Drain, then cool quickly in iced water and drain again, and spread on a clean tea towel to dry. The kernels can then be cut off the cobs, or the cobs left whole, and frozen in zip-lock bags with as much air removed as possible. Corn will keep in the freezer for up to 12 months.

See recipes on pages 236 and 258

CUCUMBERS

☀ GROWING

Cucumbers love plenty of food, water, sunshine and bees. Given all these 'ingredients', cucumbers will thrive and produce copious amounts of fruit. There are many varieties, from round to long (telegraph), to short (Lebanese). An interesting variety is the african horned, with spiked yellow skin and sweet green flesh. Then there is the lemon cucumber, shaped like a lemon with white flesh that is excellent for both salads and pickling.

For the best results, add plenty of well-rotted manure to your soil in spring or early summer. Create a mound and plant 4–5 seeds in a crater-like depression at the top. Water well, and eventually prick out the weakest seedlings, leaving the strongest 2 seedlings to scramble along the ground (or climb up a trellis if assisted with ties). Space each mound 70 cm (2 ft 4 in) apart. Keep the plants well fed and watered and pick the cucumbers regularly – they should

begin to appear about 10 weeks after planting. A handful of plants should be enough for the average family.

🦗 HARVESTING

Cucumbers can be picked as gherkins when they are very small, or grown into larger sizes for salads. Search the plants for cucumbers hiding under the foliage, and pick the cucumbers by twisting them from the plant or snipping them off with scissors.

≡ STORING

Cucumbers keep well at room temperature for 3 days or so. They can also be kept in a perforated plastic bag in the crisper for about 1 week.

Making Pickled cucumbers (see page 299) is a great way of dealing with a glut. If you're looking for something different, try roasting cucumbers. Peel them, cut in half lengthways and scoop out the seeds. Cut into pieces the shape of potato wedges. Lightly salt them and leave for 20 minutes or so to extract the excess water. Pat dry and toss with oil and herbs and bake in a hot oven for about 15 minutes. Serve hot with a knob of butter and some freshly ground pepper.

See recipes on pages 299 and 304

EGGPLANTS

☀ GROWING

Eggplants (aubergines) love a warm climate and will not tolerate cold. It takes 14–16 weeks from seed to harvest, but to get a head start you can raise them in pots under cover and transplant them outside when the soil is warmer. They enjoy full sun, lots of regular water and fertiliser and a

slightly acidic soil. Each plant will yield an average of 6–8 fruits, and staking may be necessary if the crop is heavy. Six plants should provide a family with enough fruit. Look for some of the more unusual types like Thai pea eggplants, long Lebanese eggplants, pretty striped Italian heirlooms called listada de gandia, and even baby white eggplants from where the 'egg' name first originated.

HARVESTING

The skin should be smooth, glossy and richly coloured if you are growing common purple eggplants. Snip ripe eggplants from the bush with secateurs or scissors.

≡ STORING

Eggplants can be stored at room temperature for a few days, or put in a plastic bag in the crisper to store for up to 1 week.

To freeze eggplant, cut it into 1 cm (½ in) slices and plunge into boiling water with some lemon juice added to prevent discolouration, and cook for 4 minutes. Drain and cool quickly in iced water. Drain again, spread on a clean tea towel to dry and store in zip-lock bags with as much air removed as possible. Eggplant can be frozen for up to 12 months.

See recipe on page 240

LEEKS

. . . .

☀ GROWING

Leeks are an easy vegetable to grow, surviving cold and resisting diseases and pests, plus they are flexible, being able to be harvested at a range of sizes. They are not fussy about the soil but their biggest ask is time, as they take about 6 months to grow.

Leeks are sown from seed in trays, normally in autumn, then transplanted into the ground when they are about 15 cm (6 in) tall. You should trim off the tops of the leeks to reduce transplant stress, and plant them quite deeply so that their stems start to blanch, which gives you a long and tender white stem. Deep holes are easily created using a dibbler, or alternatively a sturdy stick, and should be spaced about 15 cm (6 in) apart. After you have dropped the leeks into the holes, don't backfill – just water the seedlings well, which will wash in some soil. More soil will wash into the hole with each subsequent watering. Keep weeds away as the leeks grow, and keep building up the soil around the leeks to continue blanching, lengthening the white part of the stem.

🌱 HARVESTING

You can harvest leeks anywhere from 2 cm (¾ in) to 5 cm (2 in) thick, remembering that they are sweetest when small. Because they can be harvested at different sizes, leeks hold in the ground for a long while so you only need

to dig them out as you want them. However if you need the space, you can dig up your leeks and replant them deeply in a bunch in an unused corner of the vegetable patch and 'store' them there right up until they start to show signs of going to seed. (This is not such a bad thing if it happens – the round white or pink flower heads are quite attractive, and the seeds dropping will cause leeks to happily pop up by themselves in your patch the following season.)

To pick leeks, use a garden fork to get right under the roots to lift them without breaking their stems. Cut off the excess roots and soil with a knife.

≡ STORING

Leeks can be stored unwashed and untrimmed in a plastic bag in the crisper for about 1 week.

To freeze leeks, cut off and discard their green tops and wash the white stems carefully. Cut into rounds 4 cm (1½ in) thick. Gently fry in butter, covering with a lid and stirring occasionally, until just soft. Store the leek and fragrant butter in airtight containers in the freezer for up to 3 months. Thaw before using in soups, casseroles or pasta sauces.

See recipe on page 305

MUSHROOMS

 GROWING

While not strictly a vegetable and not grown in the soil of your garden either, mushrooms are eaten as a vegetable and are not difficult to grow. Growing kits can be purchased as a box including compost that has been inoculated with fungal spore. There are various types available – from regular white caps to swiss brown, portobello and oyster mushrooms. Once watered, 'pin heads' begin to emerge in about 2 weeks, which are ready to start cutting as button mushrooms after a few more weeks. With a sprinkle of water every few days (mushrooms need high humidity but not a lot of water), the mushrooms should continue cropping for 2–3 months.

Mushrooms will grow at any time of the year, but do best in spring and autumn. They like to be kept in the shade and out of draughts, though need ventilation. Under your house on the shadiest side or in a corner of a shed are perfect positions. Once your mushrooms have finished, spread the spent compost on your garden – it is good for any lime-loving crops, in particular broccoli, cauliflower and cabbage.

 HARVESTING

Mushrooms start as buttons, grow into cups, and finally flatten out to large field mushrooms that are perfect for stuffing. They can be picked by slicing under them with a sharp knife at any of these stages.

☰ STORING

Mushrooms should be stored in a brown paper bag on a shelf of your refrigerator (rather than in the crisper), and will keep for 5–7 days. You can wipe them clean with paper towel before you put them into the bag so they are ready to use when you need them. Mushrooms can also be frozen whole or in slices.

To dry mushrooms, thinly slice them and spread across a tray lined with baking paper. Place in an oven heated to its lowest temperature with the fan on and the door slightly ajar. Dry for 1 hour, then turn the slices and dry for another hour, until brittle. Leave to cool in the oven before storing in jars in a cool, dark place for up to 12 months, but check after a week to make sure there is no condensation. If there is, dry the mushrooms in the oven a little longer. To use, rehydrate the mushrooms in hot water for 5 minutes.

See recipe on page 204

ONICNS

 GROWING

Onions are normally sown directly from seed in autumn. Plant them into soil that has been well dug over and raked thoroughly to break up clods, with a moderate amount of complete plant food, blood and bone or pelletised chicken manure added (onions don't like to be overfed). Make rills about 6 cm (2½ in) deep, in rows about 25 cm (10 in) apart. Sprinkle seeds in but don't backfill with soil. Instead, lightly cover with some sand or vermiculite, and the soil will gradually fall back into the rills over time. Keep moist, and in a fortnight your seeds should have germinated. You can thin out the seedlings so they are spaced every 10 cm (4 in). Rows of onions totalling 6 m (20 ft) in length is a good amount for most families. Keep the weeds in control as the onions grow over the course of 6–8 months.

 HARVESTING

When the leaves start to dry off, it is time to get ready to pull up your onions. Before harvesting, clear some of the soil away from the necks of the onions and let the sun ripen their skins for 3 or 4 days. Dig them up with a shovel, then leave them outside in the sunshine for a few more days to allow their skins to dry. Rub off the dirt and excess roots, and break off the tops – unless you will be tying or braiding your onions together.

STORING

Onions are best stored hung, either tied or braided together or in mesh bags or wire baskets, so that air can flow around them. Keep in a cool, dark place for up to 6 months.

See recipes on pages 262 and 290

PEAS

GROWING

Peas are an annual plant grown from seeds sown directly into the ground in autumn and winter, and producing pods throughout winter and spring.

Like beans, peas produce their own nitrogen in nodules on their roots so don't need extra fertilising, but do like free-draining soil. Plant them in a sunny spot and water regularly, and provide a climbing structure if you are planting peas of this habit. Otherwise you can plant dwarf peas, which just grow along the ground or trail and don't need much support, so are ideal for pots and hanging baskets.

Some peas are eaten whole, such as sugar snaps and snow peas (mangetouts). All peas are fast-growing and very pretty with either white or purple flowers.

Greenfeast is a common main-crop variety, while more unusual peas include the early season, purple-podded Dutch pea capucijner and the golden-podded snow pea.

Five plants of any variety should produce around 1 kg (2 lb 3 oz) of podded peas or snow peas in a season.

Peas normally take a little encouragement to reach a trellis, so try using twigs and sticks to guide them onto their support. By around 8 weeks they should be cropping well. When the cropping has finished, dig the entire plants back into the ground to enrich your soil with organic matter and with the nitrogen that is contained in the root nodules.

HARVESTING

Pick shelling peas when the pods are not quite full (peas allowed to grow too big lose their sweetness), and go through the crop every few days as the more you pick the more you get. Snow peas should be picked by the time they are 5 cm (2 in) long and with the peas yet to swell inside the pods. Sugar snap peas should be plump and about 4 cm (1½ in) long.

For dried peas, leave some on the plant to fully ripen at the end of the season. When the leaves have withered, lift up the plant and tie upside down in a shed to dry. You can use the podded dried peas for planting next year, or you can put them in soups and stews.

The young new growth of pea plants, called pea shoots, is also edible. Pinch off 8 cm (3¼ in) lengths and add to salads or stir-fries in much the same way as you would use bean sprouts. Doing this will actually make the vines grow bushier and produce more flowers.

STORING

Eat your peas as fresh as you can, and you will notice how sweet they are. However, peas can be stored in their pods in a plastic bag in the crisper for 5 days. Shell them just before cooking.

To freeze peas, shell them and blanch for 1 minute. Drain and plunge into iced water.

Drain again, then spread over a clean tea towel to dry. Pack into zip-lock bags with as much air removed as possible and freeze for up to 12 months.

Peas can also be dried as tender young peas by picking them small and dehydrating them in the oven. **To dry young peas**, shell them and boil for 4 minutes before draining. Preheat the oven to its lowest temperature with the fan on and spread the peas over a fine-meshed wire rack set over a tray, or on a tray lined with baking paper. Leave the door slightly ajar and dry for about 8 hours, or until the peas are hard and wrinkled but still green. Leave to cool in the oven. Store in jars where they should keep for at least 12 months, but check after a week to make sure there is no condensation. If there is, dry the peas in the oven a little longer. To use the peas, soak them for 30 minutes in hot water and then simmer for around 1 hour.

See recipe on page 203

RHUBARB

GROWING

Established gardens often have rhubarb growing somewhere, as it is a hardy perennial vegetable that even tolerates semi-shade, though it grows best in the sun. The plant has huge, dark green leaves atop long green or red stems that make it a particularly pretty addition to the vegetable patch. The leaves are actually poisonous, but the tender stems are excellent for cooking.

You can get started by buying crowns in winter, which are often wrapped in wood shavings in a net bag, or otherwise purchase selected varieties in pots at any time of the year. You can also divide an established plant yourself in late winter or early spring. Allow about 1 m (3 ft 4 in) square per plant and make sure you prepare the bed well, removing all weeds and working in some well-rotted manure and complete plant food, too – remember, your plant is going to be there for a while and you want to give it the best home possible. Rhubarb responds well to regular applications of liquid fertiliser like seaweed solution or fish emulsion.

HARVESTING

Rhubarb can be harvested in its second year of growth. Stems are usually pulled in spring through to early summer, from the outside of the plant in. Hold towards the base of the stem and simply pull it outwards, giving a slight twist. Always leave at least a few stems on the plant. Put the leaves in the compost.

In winter rhubarb dies back in cold climates, and grows more slowly in others – but you can force an early crop of rhubarb by covering it with a terracotta bell jar (called a forcing jar) or a box. This brings on tender growth by keeping out the cold and the light, but you should only do this to a plant every few years.

≡ STORING

Rhubarb keeps well in a plastic bag in the crisper for 2–3 weeks. It also freezes well – cut it into lengths and blanch for 1 minute before cooling in iced water, draining and spreading on a clean tea towel to dry. Pack into zip-lock bags, removing as much air as possible, and freeze for up to 6 months. Rhubarb is commonly stewed with sugar, which can be refrigerated for a week or so or frozen for up to 12 months, or put in sterilised jars and heat-processed (see page 12) if desired.

See recipes on pages 185 and 280

TOMATOES

☀ GROWING

As a general rule of thumb, tomatoes do well in soil that has just grown a leafy green crop as it will have extracted the excess nitrogen. Tomatoes are heavy feeders, but nitrogen in particular just promotes tomatoes to grow leaves. (In turn, root vegetables such as carrots and onions are good for following tomatoes, as they are not nutrient hungry. Legumes such as peas can be next, as they bring nitrogen to the soil, with leafy greens afterwards – followed by fruiting plants such as tomatoes again. Of course, you always need to add organic matter to the soil and feed plants based on their needs.)

Tomatoes come in a wide range of varieties, from cherry tomatoes to round salad tomatoes, to roma (plum) tomatoes that are used for pastes and sauces. Some ripen red; others yellow, white, striped or almost black. They all need a sunny position and should be planted in spring when the frosts have finished. They are happy in the garden or in a pot, so long as they have regular watering.

Most tomatoes need staking but some are stockier, which are ideal for pots, while some are even trailing and can be used to tumble over pots or hanging baskets. Grafted tomatoes are available and tend to be heavy bearers, producing up to 10 kg (22 lb) of fruit per plant. Tomatoes vary in the time it takes until harvest, with the smaller types ready as early as 8 weeks and the larger ones at about 12 weeks.

There are different ways of growing tomatoes, but one way is to plant them 50 cm (20 in) apart and pinch out the laterals (the small shoots that emerge at the joints) to leave one central stem, and keep the leaves down to about 7 or 8 branches on the plant, removing them from the ground up as the plant grows. To protect developing fruit from fruit fly, consider placing each truss in a sheer organza bag once it starts to colour. You can buy these in party stores and from some seed suppliers.

🐦 HARVESTING

Some varieties ripen almost all at once, such as the popular grosse lisse. Other varieties such as cherry types will bear throughout the season, so it's important to consider what you want before planting. Tomatoes ripen quickly in summer and you will need to inspect your plants every few days, picking the ripe ones as you see them as they can fall quickly. Try to pick your tomatoes with the green calyx and short stem attached as this helps them keep longer.

⬛ STORING

Fresh tomatoes store best at room temperature and should be kept away from other fruits such as bananas, which accelerate their ripening. They should keep for at least a few days.

Small tomatoes can be frozen whole – place them on a tray lined with baking paper and when they are frozen hard, transfer into zip-lock bags removing as much air as possible. Freeze for up to 12 months. You can cook them straight from frozen. Large tomatoes are better for making passata (see page 316).

When peeling tomatoes, you don't have to waste the skins – use them to make **tomato powder or flakes**. Put the skins on a tray lined with baking paper and place in an oven heated to its lowest temperature, with the fan on and the door slightly ajar. Dry until crisp, then cool and pop into a spice grinder to blitz to a powder, or use a food processor to make flakes. Store in a jar and use like you would paprika, only to add a tomatoey zest.

To dry tomatoes, cut them in half and spread them skin-side down over fine-meshed wire racks set on trays. (If you only have racks with wide gaps, then line the racks with aluminium foil and prick all over with a fork.) Sprinkle a little salt over the tomatoes. Place in an oven heated to its lowest temperature with the fan on and the door slightly ajar. Dry for anywhere between 6 and 12 hours, depending on the size of the pieces, until the tomatoes have a leathery feel a bit like a raisin. Leave the tomatoes in the oven to cool before putting into jars. Check after a week to make sure there is no condensation – if there is, dry the tomatoes in the oven a little longer. (In warm, dry areas, you can dry tomatoes in the sun with a layer of muslin/cheesecloth on top to keep off the bugs, but this takes 1–2 weeks of sunny weather, and the trays need to be brought in at night.) Dried tomatoes should keep in a cool, dark place for up to 12 months or in the freezer for up to 18 months. Add them to soups and stews or cover with olive oil to rehydrate them and serve as an antipasto.

See recipes on pages 197, 210, 216, 222, 226, 244, 246, 258, 316, 318 and 329

ZUCCHINI

☀ GROWING

Zucchini (courgettes) like to be grown with lots of food and water and plenty of summer sunshine. Liquid manure works well and can be applied every 2–3 weeks. Zucchini are normally grown on top of a small mound to encourage good drainage, and planted from seed once there is no more chance of frost in spring. They take about 6–8 weeks from seed until they start cropping, and bear prolifically, producing an average of 3 kg (6 lb 10 oz) of fruit per plant, depending on the variety. The fruit can grow into large marrows if you let it. Bees are needed for pollinating as the plants

have male and female flowers, so you should encourage bees into your vegetable patch by not spraying, and by planting flowers. Zucchini flowers are edible and popular for stuffing, and in fact the new shoots and young leaves are edible too, steamed or stir-fried. Tromboncino is an interesting climbing zucchini that has a bulbous end, and costata romanesco is a heavily ribbed heirloom variety.

🏃 HARVESTING

Look carefully for zucchini as they do hide behind those enormous leaves. Fruit of around 10–15 cm (4–6 in) has the best flavour. Give the zucchini a gentle twist to remove them from the plant. If picking flowers, pick them in the morning or evening and pinch out the pistil or stamen before cooking.

≡ STORING

Zucchini will keep fresh in a perforated plastic bag in the crisper for 1 week. **To freeze zucchini**, cut them into 2 cm (¾ in) rounds and blanch for a few minutes. Drain and cool in iced water, then drain again and spread on a clean tea towel to dry. Pack into zip-lock bags removing as much air as possible and freeze for up to 12 months.

See recipes on pages 253 and 295

HERB
GARDEN

BASIL

—·—

GROWING

Basil comes in a range of varieties, from the usual sweet basil to lemon, purple, Thai, Greek and lettuce leaf. Almost all are annuals, although there is also a much hardier perennial basil worth seeking out.

Basil likes a sunny spot in rich and free-draining but moist soil. Seeds can be sown outdoors as soon as the weather warms up and the chance of frost has passed. Alternatively, you can get a head start by raising seedlings in pots indoors. As plants grow, pinch out the centre bud to encourage branching. Keep removing the flower buds as they form too, as this will encourage more leaf growth.

HARVESTING

Basil can be picked leaf by leaf at any time of the day, but if you are harvesting larger amounts, then go out in the morning and cut up to a third off the top of each plant, cutting cleanly just above a leaf pair. At the end of the season, be sure to pick all your basil before the first frost, as otherwise the leaves blacken and are wasted.

≡ STORING

Fresh basil lasts about 1 week with its stems placed in a glass of water and the whole

lot placed in a plastic bag to create a mini glasshouse, stored in the refrigerator.

Basil can be made into butters or pestos and kept for a short time in the refrigerator, or for longer in the freezer.

To dry basil, wash and remove any dead or spotted leaves from the plants, and either hang the plants upside down in bunches, or pick the leaves and spread them in a single layer on trays lined with baking paper and leave in a dark, well-ventilated place for about a week until completely dry. Crumble the leaves or keep them whole and use the paper to tip the basil into jars. Store in a cool, dark place for up to 12 months.

See recipes on pages 182, 198, 202 and 271

BAY

☀ GROWING

Bay is easy to grow and can be planted in the ground or kept in pots – if in pots, it is best to re-pot every few years. It has creamy yellow flowers in spring, but it is the dark green, leathery leaves that are the hero. The leaves will have the highest oil content and best flavour when the plant is grown in full sun.

Bay is actually a tree that grows around 8 m (26 ft) tall, but can be kept pruned or topiarised into shapes, and these are sometimes featured

outside restauraunts as 'standards'.

Feed bay with controlled-release fertiliser once a year and don't let the plant dry out through summer. Watch for scale insects and use white oil if necessary.

 HARVESTING

Pick leaves that are dark green, rather than any new, lighter growth. It is best to pick leaves when the plant is dry, and make sure the leaves are free of scale.

≡ STORING

You can wrap fresh bay leaves in damp paper towel, place in a plastic bag and store in the refrigerator for up to 2 weeks.

To dry bay leaves, place them in a single layer on trays lined with baking paper and leave them in a warm, well-ventilated place out of direct sunlight for about 2 weeks, turning them after a week. Once there is no sign of green left, the leaves are ready for putting in jars. Store in a cool, dark place for up to 12 months.

To infuse vodka with bay leaves, blanch about 6 leaves in boiling water, then put them into a sterilised bottle. Cover with 750 ml (25 fl oz/3 cups) of vodka and leave to infuse for 1 month before removing the leaves. The essential oil from the bay leaves gives the vodka a herbal flavour.

CHIVES

GROWING

Chives are a member of the onion family and have a delightful light onion-like flavour. They are a hardy perennial growing to about 30 cm (1 ft) tall in full sun, just about anywhere from very cold to warmer areas, although they die back in winter in colder climates. They can be sown from seed or division, simply cutting up established clumps with a spade and transplanting them to new homes. The key is drainage, so if you don't have beds that are naturally well draining, either make a raised bed or grow chives in pots. The flowers are also edible. Watch out for thrips and aphids, and consider a soap spray if these become a problem. Feed with pelletised manure.

HARVESTING

Chives should be picked with scissors or a sharp knife by bunching stems together and cutting them off no closer than about 4 cm (1½ in) from the base. The leaves will grow again like hair, but always try to cut from a new area of the plant each time. If you live in a cold area, you might want to cut the whole clump at the end of autumn before it dies back of its own accord and freeze or dry some chives for use over winter.

☰ STORING

Wrap fresh chives in damp paper towel, put inside a plastic bag and store in the refrigerator for up to 1 week. For longer storage chives can be frozen, dried or blended with butter. When frozen, chives defrost quite well as the hollow stems resist collapsing.

To freeze chives, chop them into about 1 cm (½ in) lengths. Put into ice-cube trays and add a little water. Once frozen, transfer into zip-lock bags and store for up to 6 months. To use, simply defrost and drain.

To dry chives, spread chopped chives on trays lined with baking paper and dry in an oven heated to its lowest temperature, with the fan on and the door slightly ajar. It normally takes about 2 hours until the chives are dry and crumbly. Once dry, you can break the chives into smaller flakes if desired, and use the paper to tip the chives into a jar. Store in a cool, dark place for up to 12 months.

Chive butter is perfect for spreading on bread, scones, potatoes and steak, and can be stored in the refrigerator or frozen – see the recipe on page 208.

See recipes on pages 198 and 208

CORIANDER

GROWING

Coriander (cilantro) is edible in its entirety, from the roots and leaves to the flowers and seeds. It has been used both medicinally and in cooking for millennium, but has become very popular in the last few decades.

Find a full-sun (winter) or partially shaded (summer) position that drains well, and add lots of compost. Rake the soil over so that all rocks and clods are removed. Coriander is best grown from seed as any change of position can cause it to bolt. It is also best planted every few weeks from early spring throughout summer and autumn, thus growing a small but continual harvest of the leaves. Coriander should be fed with liquid fertiliser every 2 weeks or so.

HARVESTING

Coriander leaves are best before the plant begins to bolt, as the leaves then change flavour and become less palatable. Pick coriander in the morning or evening rather than in the heat of the day, and use a sharp pair of scissors, cutting the foliage from the outside. Alternatively, you can pull coriander plants up root and all.

All is not lost when coriander bolts, as the flowers attract beneficial insects and the seeds are of course also edible. Once these have formed, place a brown paper bag over the top of the plant and secure with a rubber band.

Cut the stem and hang it upside down in a dry, dark place for a few weeks and the bag will catch the seeds as they fall.

STORING

Fresh coriander lasts about 2 weeks with its stems placed in a glass of water and the whole lot placed in a plastic bag to create a mini glasshouse, stored in the refrigerator.

To freeze coriander, quickly blanch it, refresh it in iced water and pat it dry before freezing in zip-lock bags with as much air removed as possible. Another method is to process blanched leaves with a little oil to make a simple pesto without nuts. You can freeze this into ice-cube trays, transferring to zip-lock bags when frozen.

Alternatively, chop blanched coriander and mix it with butter (about 1 part leaves to 4 parts butter) and store it in the refrigerator for a few weeks, or cut it into portions and freeze. With each method coriander will keep in the freezer for around 3 months, and the blanching prevents the leaves from blackening in the freezer.

See recipes on pages 192 and 195

CURRY LEAVES

 ## GROWING

Some might say that curry leaf is the magic ingredient of curries from southern India. The small, deep green leaflets grow in a neat pattern on a central stem, and are traditionally fried to release their flavour in dishes, although fresh leaves can also be dried for adding to soups and stews.

The tree grows to about 3 m (10 ft) tall and tends to produce suckers. It comes from the tropics and subtropics and likes a warm position free of heavy frost. It can be grown in pots or in the ground, where it can reach 4–6 m (13–20 ft) tall, though is usually much smaller and can be pruned to stay compact. The tree appreciates lots of water and feeding, but will survive on less once established.

 ## STORING

Wrap fresh curry leaves in damp paper towel, place inside a plastic bag and store in the refrigerator for up to 1 week.

To freeze curry leaves, just package the leaves in zip-lock bags with as much air removed as possible. They will easily keep in the freezer for 3 months or so and will retain good flavour.

To dry curry leaves, spread them on a tray lined with baking paper and place in an oven heated to its lowest temperature, with the fan on and the door slightly ajar. Dry for 1–2 hours, until brittle. Crumble the leaves or keep them whole and use the paper to tip them into a jar. Store in a cool, dark place for up to 12 months.

 ## HARVESTING

About 20 leaves are usually enough for a curry, and it is best to snip off a sprig or two just before use. In colder climates, pick some leaves for freezing or drying at the end of autumn before they yellow.

DILL

☀ GROWING

Dill can be one of the most frustrating plants to grow, but its flavour is unique and both the leaves and seeds are delicious, so it's worth persisting. The problem with dill is its habit of bolting to seed so quickly that you haven't had time to harvest much foliage. You can get around this by staggering your planting, and only growing it from seed sown directly into your garden beds, as dill hates to be transplanted as a seedling. Sow from early spring through to early summer, planting 6 or 8 plants every 4 weeks. You can forget about growing dill in the heat of summer – but resume sowing in mid-autumn when the weather starts to cool again. You can normally get another 2 sowings in before winter arrives. Dill likes free-draining soil and a regular application of liquid fertiliser every 2–3 weeks.

 HARVESTING

Handle dill with care as it bruises easily. Pick early in the morning using scissors, and remove any damaged or discoloured leaves, choosing only fresh sprigs.

To pick dill for drying, wait for the plant to bolt and cut the stem just before the flowers open, as the oil content of the leaves is at its highest at this point.

If you want to collect the seeds, allow the plant to flower and the seed heads to brown.

Place a brown paper bag over the top of the plant and secure with a rubber band. Cut the stem and hang it upside down in a dry, dark place for a few weeks and the bag will catch the seeds as they fall.

☰ STORING

To keep dill fresh, wash it and wrap it in damp paper towel and place inside a plastic bag – it will store in the refrigerator for up to 5 days.

To dry dill, remove any woody stems and wash and dry the sprigs, then snip into 3 cm (1¼ in) lengths. Spread on a tray lined with baking paper. Place in an oven heated to its lowest temperature with the fan on and the door slightly ajar and dry for 30 minutes. Check if the dill is dry – if not, continue drying a little longer. Crumble the dill and use the paper to tip it into a jar. Store in a cool, dark place for up to 12 months.

Store dill seeds in a jar and keep in the refrigerator for maximum freshness. Use them in savoury biscuits or on loaves of bread, or toast them and sprinkle over salads or creamy soups.

See recipe on page 208

ELDERFLOWERS AND ELDERBERRIES

GROWING

Few plants could be as trouble free or adaptable as elder, which grows in almost any climate, from cool mountain areas to the subtropics. The lacy white flowers look like doilies and the berries hang in large clusters like jewels. It likes a sunny position and will flower freely and produce many kilos of fruit per plant, especially after good rains. The shrub grows to about 3 m (10 ft) tall in any soil and is hardy to frost. There are very pretty forms with golden or variegated leaves, and even one with purple leaves. Elder lasts about 10 years and can be grown from cuttings to replenish stocks. (Please note that while the flowers and berries are edible, the leaves, branches and roots of the plant are toxic.)

HARVESTING

When harvesting the flowers, they are best picked on a dry sunny day when the natural yeasts are about in the pollen.

Elderberries grow in clusters and are ripe when shiny and violet. Cut off whole clusters, then remove the berries from their stalks over a bowl, using a fork to gently coax them off.

While elderberries are highly nutritious when fully ripe, it is not recommended that you eat more than a few berries at a time due to a small amount of toxins they contain. Cooking the berries, even just slightly, removes all toxins.

STORING

Elderflowers, with their sweet, floral flavour, are best used straight after picking, such as in cordial (see page 168). Many wines and champagnes are also made utilising the natural yeasts in the flowers. These can then be made into lovely vinegar.

Elderberries, which have a similar flavour to blackcurrants, can be stored in the refrigerator for up to 2 weeks, or frozen for up to 6 months. They can be made into a different version of cordial (see page 168), or into syrups, jellies or pies.

See recipe on page 168

GARLIC

 GROWING

Garlic is a cool-season crop that takes 6–8 months to be ready for harvest. But it doesn't take up a lot of space and you can easily grow a year's supply in one good row.

Prepare your soil before planting by making sure it is crumbly, free of weeds and stones, and has good drainage. Dig in some manure. Plant out your cloves in late winter and early spring, or if you live in an area where winter is not severe, and if your soil is not too wet, autumn sowing is also possible, giving the crop a good head start and making for fatter, fuller bulbs.

Start by creating a continuous rill about 4 cm (1½ in) deep using the edge of a steel rake or a hoe, or just a hand shovel. Plant each individual clove about 10 cm (4 in) apart, cover with soil and then start your next row about 30 cm (1 ft) away. Keep the garlic well watered and weeded.

 HARVESTING

Garlic is ready to be harvested when the tops begin yellowing. When this happens, carefully hoe back some of the soil from the ripening bulbs to let the sun shine on their skins for 3 or 4 days. This will help mature the bulbs and thicken their skins. Pull up your garlic by carefully lifting under the bulbs with a garden fork.

☰ STORING

Garlic is traditionally plaited together by its withering stems and hung. You can also just tie the stems together with string, or put the bulbs in mesh bags for hanging. Store in a cool, dry place for up to 6 months. After a while, when the season changes and the temperatures drop, garlic will begin to sprout, and you can preserve your remaining garlic by making Garlic confit (see page 322).

To smoke garlic, place whole bulbs with a little olive oil and salt on pieces of aluminium foil and wrap well into individual parcels so that all the juices will stay inside. Place the parcels inside a smoker, or use a wood-fired barbecue with a lid and put some damp woodchips onto the fire when it is low and smouldering. This will create steam as well as smoke. Put the lid on and smoke the garlic for 30–40 minutes. Leave to cool before separating into cloves, putting into sterilised jars and covering with olive oil. Store in the refrigerator for up to 1 month. To use, just squeeze the garlic out of its skins. Smoked garlic is sensational with anything – try it with something simple where you really notice the flavour, such as with boiled potatoes, in green salads or smeared on toast!

See recipe on page 322

GINGER

 GROWING

Ginger is commercially grown in the tropics where it can produce many rhizomes each year. The large, slightly palm-like green leaves that reach about 80 cm (2 ft 8 in) tall, as well as the torch-like flowers, make it a very pretty plant.

The home gardener can expect about 15 cm (6 in) of rhizome from a single plant in the first year, and double that in subsequent years when the clump is established. The plant's leaves die back in late autumn.

In frost-free areas you should plant ginger in a free-draining soil in a warm and sheltered position in spring. If you live in a cooler area you can try growing ginger in a pot, and you should harvest your ginger before any frost. If leaving some ginger in the pot for regrowing, move the pot under cover for winter.

You can simply plant ginger bought from the greengrocer – just break off a knob. Feed regularly and make sure you keep the water up, although ginger can cope with drying out over winter when dormant.

HARVESTING

Late autumn when the foliage yellows is the time to harvest mature ginger. Use a garden fork to loosen the surrounding soil and lift up some rhizomes. Cut these off with a knife.

If you have an established plant, you can also harvest young rhizomes during summer from the edge of the clump. This ginger has thinner skin, is more delicate, and doesn't keep long, but has a delicious, fresh flavour to it.

STORING

Wash and dry ginger, then store it unwrapped in a cool, dark place where it will keep for many weeks. Alternatively, store it in a plastic bag in the refrigerator for 1–2 months. Ginger can also be frozen either grated or whole for up to 12 months – if grated you can use it straight from the freezer.

To dry ginger, grate it and spread it across a tray lined with baking paper. Place in an oven heated to its lowest temperature with the fan on and the door slightly ajar and dry for about 1 hour, or until completely dehydrated. Leave to cool in the oven, then store in a jar in a cool, dark place for up to 12 months.

To cook ginger in syrup, make a syrup with 1 part caster (superfine) sugar to 2 parts water. Add ginger chopped up into 2 cm (¾ in) chunks and simmer for about 20 minutes, until translucent. Spoon the hot ginger and syrup into warm sterilised jars and seal. Store in a cool, dark place for up to 12 months. You can use the ginger in baking, and the syrup as cordial with soda water (club soda) or served on ice-cream. It's also delicious in cake frosting, especially on carrot cakes or fruit muffins.

Young ginger can be pickled (see page 292).

See recipes on pages 259 and 292

HORSERADISH

☀ GROWING

Horseradish is a very hardy plant that can easily become invasive, spreading by root division. It is these roots that the plant is mostly grown for – they grow from spring until autumn, and are dug up in autumn unless you have a mature clump, in which case they can be dug as needed. However, tender young horseradish leaves, which look a bit like spinach, are also delicious steamed or stir-fried.

You can buy potted horseradish plants and plant them out year round, or dig up a root from an existing plant in late winter just before the new leaves sprout. Plant about 30 cm (1 ft) apart in just about any type of soil that has been well dug over. Horseradish needs at least half a day's sun, but will tolerate quite cold overnight temperatures. It likes regular water. If you're worried about it spreading out of control, either plant it in large troughs or use a root control barrier in your garden.

 HARVESTING

Horseradish leaves can be picked when young and tender using scissors. The roots can be harvested by gently loosening the surrounding soil with a garden fork and carefully levering roots out.

≡ STORING

Fresh horseradish can be stored in a box of dry sand in a cool, dark place for up to 3 months. Alternatively, you can store it in a perforated plastic bag in the crisper for 1–2 weeks. To use horseradish, just peel and grate the root (you can wear glasses or even swimming goggles to keep your eyes from watering). The grated horseradish can be mixed with vinegar and stored in a jar in the refrigerator for up to 1 month. Washed and trimmed whole roots can also be frozen for up to 6 months.

To dry horseradish, grate it and spread it across a tray lined with baking paper. Place in an oven heated to its lowest temperature with the fan on and the door slightly ajar and dry for about 1 hour, or until completely dehydrated. Leave to cool in the oven, then store in a jar in a cool, dark place for up to 12 months. You can use the flakes in stews and soups, or rehydrate them in a little hot water and mix with vinegar and sour cream for horseradish sauce.

See recipe on page 231

KAFFIR LIME

☀ GROWING

Kaffir lime is normally grown for its delicious double leaves rather than its fruit, which have gnarled skin and are edible like a regular lime, although they are not very juicy. The plants are intolerant of cold, but can be grown in a pot in a cooler climate as long as you move them under cover to give them frost protection over winter. Spraying with a product called DroughtShield will also help protect them from frost burn.

In the ground kaffir limes grow to around 3 x 3 m (10 x 10 ft). Feed them in autumn and spring with complete plant food, and throw on some slow-release or pelletised manure as well, as they are heavy feeders. Mulch well, but be careful to avoid the trunk as they can get collar rot.

🐦 HARVESTING

The best leaves to pick are those that are full size and no longer pale green, but rather have turned a rich dark green. These mature leaves don't wilt as quickly and have a rich oil content, which is what gives them their flavour.

≡ STORING

Put kaffir lime leaves in a zip-lock bag with as much air removed as possible and store in the refrigerator for up to 2 weeks or in the freezer for up to 12 months.

LEMONGRASS

☀ GROWING

The strappy foliage of lemongrass grows to about 1 m (3 ft 4 in) tall and makes an interesting addition to the herb garden, where many plants are ground covers, small annuals or shrubs. It's a tropical plant, so in cold areas it is treated as an annual and planted in spring, or it can be grown in a pot and then moved under cover before the first frost. It loves lots of water and regular feeding with pelletised manure or liquid fertiliser. You can strike lemongrass from a shop-bought stalk – just put it in a glass of water to root before planting out. After about 2 years this can grow to a clump producing about 20 stems each season.

🌿 HARVESTING

Lemongrass stalks are harvested once they are over 1 cm (½ in) thick. In warm climates you can harvest any time of year, while in cooler areas you need to harvest all your stalks before winter hits, or move your plant to a protected position under cover if growing in a pot.

The stalks are cut off at ground level with a knife or twisted firmly, from the outside of the plant. Remove the outer woody layers and the leaves – the leaves can be dried if desired.

☰ STORING

Lemongrass stalks can be wrapped in damp paper towel and stored in a plastic bag in the refrigerator for up to 2 weeks. They can also be cut into pencil lengths and frozen in zip-lock bags with as much air removed as possible for up to 12 months.

To dry lemongrass leaves, roughly chop up the entire leaves (reserving the white stalks for cooking) and place on a fine-meshed wire rack in the sun for about 8 hours, until crisp. Alternatively, spread them on a tray lined with baking paper and dry for a few hours in an oven heated to its lowest temperature, with the fan on and the door slightly ajar. Crumble the leaves and store in jars in a cool, dark place for up to 12 months. Use to flavour stews and soups, sprinkle on fish, or just steep in boiling water for a cup of lemongrass tea.

See recipes on pages 180 and 192

LEMON MYRTLE

 GROWING

This Australian native is an excellent alternative to lemon-like herbs such as lemon verbena, and in fact it has the highest level of citral oil of any plant known. The fresh leaves can be used in curries as you would use bay or kaffir lime, or added to cakes and desserts.

The tree comes from the rainforests of Queensland, but grows happily in any frost-free area or in a warm microclimate. It has creamy flowers in autumn and when you brush past the leaves or after rain you get a wonderful sherbet fragrance. Lemon myrtle makes a lovely screen or tall hedge and it's perfect for that shady spot between houses where you want to block out the neighbours. You might want to prune the tree regularly as it can grow to about 8 m (26 ft).

Lemon myrtle loves a humus-rich soil with lots of compost and regular water. It will grow in the shade, but prefers some sunshine to really bring out the flavour in its leaves. It appreciates a thick layer of mulch to stop the surface roots from drying out.

 HARVESTING

Pick growth that's hardened off as it is richer in oil and less likely to wilt. You can cut branches up to 60 cm (2 ft) long.

STORING

Fresh leaves can be put into zip-lock bags with as much air removed as possible and stored in the refrigerator for up to 1 week, or in the freezer for up to 12 months.

To dry lemon myrtle, tie branches together and hang upside down in a dry place with plenty of air circulation. Alternatively, strip the leaves from the branches and hang in a clean hessian bag. Once the leaves are brittle, they can be broken into flakes for tea (just add hot water), or milled in a spice grinder to make a powder for seasoning. Store in a jar in a cool, dark place for up to 12 months.

To make lemon myrtle syrup, cover about 12 roughly chopped fresh leaves with 250 ml (8½ fl oz/1 cup) of boiling water and leave to steep. Once cool, strain into a saucepan, discarding the leaves, and add 230 g (8 oz/ 1 cup) of caster (superfine) sugar. Bring to the boil, stirring until the sugar dissolves, then lower the heat and simmer until syrupy and reduced by about a third. Store in a sterilised bottle in the refrigerator for up to 12 months and add to icings for biscuits and cakes, or use to flavour sorbet.

To infuse vodka with lemon myrtle, follow the directions for vodka with bay leaves on page 114.

See recipe on page 248

MINT

GROWING

Mint can be sweet, spicy, chocolatey or just plain minty depending on the variety. It is a perennial, spreading plant, rooting wherever it touches the ground, which is why many people grow it in pots. Otherwise, mint is best planted in a contained area of the garden where spreading won't be a problem. It grows to about 30 cm (1 ft) tall and has edible mauve flowers.

Mint can be grown in many climates and its main requirement is moisture. It doesn't cope with drying out, so it is best planted in a wet patch where water is reliable. It can even be grown in pots that have their bases submerged in a pond so water can be drawn up freely.

Mint can cope with either sun or shade. Soil enriched with manure or compost is best and the plant does well with an annual application of lime. Mint is prone to rust, so cut it back hard if this occurs to make way for new growth.

HARVESTING

Cut mint early in the morning or late in the afternoon when it is fresh and not wilted. Use scissors to avoid ripping it out of the ground.

☰ STORING

Fresh mint lasts about 2 weeks with its stems placed in a glass of water and the whole lot placed in a plastic bag to create a mini glasshouse, stored in the refrigerator.

To freeze mint, follow the directions for coriander (cilantro) on page 118.

To dry mint, follow the directions for sage on page 152, or pick the leaves and spread them in a single layer on trays lined with baking paper and leave in a dark, well-ventilated place for about 1 week, until completely dry. Crumble the leaves or keep them whole and tip into jars. Store in a cool, dark place for up to 12 months.

To make mint sorbet, combine 230 g (8 oz/1 cup) of caster (superfine) sugar, 500 ml (17 fl oz/2 cups) of water and 12 mint leaves in a saucepan, stirring until the sugar dissolves. Bring to the boil, then remove from the heat and leave to cool. Discard the mint leaves and pour the syrup into a wide metal tray. Freeze until just set. Use a food processor to blend the sorbet to a smooth texture, then refreeze it in an airtight container, where it can be stored in the freezer for up to 6 months. Before serving, whip 2 egg whites to stiff peaks in a food processor. Add the sorbet in pieces and blend together. Refreeze for another few hours and serve as a palate cleanser or dessert.

See recipes on pages 164, 200, 203 and 210

OREGANO
AND MARJORAM

GROWING

Oregano is a hardy ground cover with slightly woody stems and soft and flavoursome new growth. There are many varieties, from golden and variegated to Greek and za'atar. Closely related marjoram has smaller leaves that are slightly softer and sweeter.

Oregano and marjoram thrive in an open, sunny position where they can develop their full flavour. Drainage is paramount, so rockeries and between paving are ideal, and a coarse sandy or gravelly soil is perfect. Most varieties are sensitive to frost and they don't like too much humidity, either. Pots are perfect for cool areas as plants can be moved under cover during winter. Don't overfeed, and keep the plants well trimmed so they remain vigorous.

HARVESTING

Use scissors to snip oregano and marjoram in the morning, after any dew has dried from the leaves. The flavour of the leaves is at its peak before the flowers open. The flowers are edible too. Long stems can be harvested in autumn and are useful as skewers either fresh or dried.

 STORING

To keep oregano or marjoram fresh, wash it, wrap it in damp paper towel and place inside a plastic bag – it can be stored in the refrigerator for up to 1 week.

To freeze oregano or marjoram, pick the leaves from the stems, wash them, and pat them dry. Spread in a single layer over a tray lined with baking paper and freeze. Once frozen, transfer to zip-lock bags with as much air removed as possible and it should keep for many months.

To dry oregano or marjoram (the flowers can be dried too), follow the directions for sage on page 152.

PARSLEY

 GROWING

Parsley is best grown from seed sown directly into the garden so it won't suffer from transplant shock and bolt into flower. Any time from mid-winter (in mild areas) to early summer is suitable. It likes a sunny position but can tolerate half a day's shade, and prefers well-drained soil though it also likes regular water. A few parsley plants are enough for most families. The main forms are curly and flat-leaf (Italian) – both taste better the faster you grow them, so feed them every 3 weeks with a liquid fertiliser like seaweed solution up until the plants begin to go to seed. Parsley will self-seed in the garden if you let it – if you do, it will be there almost whenever you need it. The flowers also attract beneficial insects.

HARVESTING

Just use scissors and clip at the base of each stem. Harvest before flowers begin forming as then the leaves start to become bitter.

STORING

You can keep bunches of parsley quite well just by sitting them in a glass of water. They last even longer if you place a plastic bag around both the glass and the parsley like a greenhouse and keep this in the refrigerator.

The best way of freezing parsley is to process leaves with a little oil to make a simple pesto without nuts. Freeze in ice-cube trays, transferring to zip-lock bags when frozen, and store for up to 3 months.

To dry parsley, spread leaves on trays lined with baking paper and dry in an oven heated to its lowest temperature with the fan on and the door slightly ajar. It normally takes about 2 hours until the parsley is dry and crumbly. Once dry, break into smaller flakes if desired and use the paper to tip the parsley into a jar. Store in a cool, dark place for up to 12 months.

See recipes on pages 195 and 198

PERILLA

 ## GROWING

Also called shiso, this annual herb is closely related to mint and basil, and is one of the essential herbs in Japanese and Korean cooking – Koreans put it to great use in perilla kimchi. There is both green and red perilla, each with a unique flavour, just as basil varieties taste subtly different.

Find a warm place in the garden to sow seeds in spring, or raise seedlings in trays if preferred. Space plants about 30 cm (1 ft) apart, and start picking once the plants have at least 12 leaves. Keep the plants moist and use plenty of liquid fertiliser as they grow. Pinch out the tips to encourage bushy growth and to keep the plants from flowering.

 ## HARVESTING

The leaves wilt easily, so it's best to take a bucket of water out into the garden while picking, popping the stems straight into the bucket.

 ## STORING

If you have both green and red perilla, store and prepare them separately as they can discolour each other. You can keep them fresh in the refrigerator for a few days wrapped in damp paper towel inside a plastic bag.

To freeze perilla, quickly blanch the leaves in boiling water, then plunge into iced water to cool. Drain and pat dry, and freeze in zip-lock bags with as much air removed as possible for up to 3 months.

To marinate perilla in soy and garlic, blanch the leaves as for freezing, then put into an airtight container, drizzle with soy sauce and add a small clove of garlic. Leave to marinate at room temperature for 1 day before transferring to the refrigerator. Marinated perilla keeps for about 1 month and is delicious with sashimi and sushi.

To preserve perilla in salt, wash the leaves then drain and dry on a clean tea towel. Scatter some salt in the bottom of an airtight container then add a single layer of leaves. Follow with a thin layer of salt, then more leaves and continue to layer. Put on the lid and leave in the refrigerator for a few days before using, and consume within 1–2 weeks. The salted leaves can be used instead of nori sheets (just dust off the excess salt), or shredded and tossed through hot noodles. They can also be blitzed in a food processor – salt and all – into a powder as a topping for rice and other things. The flavoured salt, either with or without the leaves, is also a delicious rub for fish.

Perilla leaves can also be preserved in brine in much the same way as vine leaves.

See recipe on page 333

ROCKET

 ## GROWING

One of the easiest salad leaves to grow, rocket (arugula) will be a great standby once you have it established in the garden, as there are always leaves ready to eat if you let some plants go to seed. The seeds disperse and plants continue to pop up.

Rocket only takes about 4 weeks from seed until you can start harvesting. To get it started, plant seeds directly into well-drained, friable soil or into a pot. It can be planted in full or part sun – needing at least half a day's sunshine for good flavour – and it responds well to liquid feeding once established. Rocket can be grown at virtually any time of the year and is not fussy about the climate.

 ## HARVESTING

Picking a few leaves from several plants is preferable to decimating one bush for the night's salad. Pick from the outside of the plants using scissors or by pinching off leaves with your fingertips.

When rocket starts to form flower stems, the leaves become bitter rather than sweet and nutty as they are when young. But you can cut the plant back hard several times and it will reshoot with fresh batches of leaves. If you do leave your rocket to flower and go to seed, you can also enjoy the flowers as they are edible too.

STORING

Rocket is best picked straight from the garden, although you can wash it and store it in a plastic bag in the crisper for 3–4 days.

See recipe on page 202

ROSELLA

 ## GROWING

Rosella is an annual plant that quickly grows into a bush 2 m (6½ ft) high through the warm months. It needs about 6 months of warm weather and is not recommended for cool climates. Its hibiscus-like flowers are edible and can be used in salads. The tender young leaves can be eaten as a steamed green too, but it is the fleshy red calyx that forms around a green seed pod several weeks after the flowers fall that is used to make rosella jam or rosellas in syrup, which are popular mixed with sparkling wines, and are also dried to make tea. The seeds germinate best if first soaked in warm water for 1 hour. Then you plant them directly into an open sunny position with well-drained soil and space to grow.

 ## HARVESTING

Young and juicy rosellas are the best, as older ones can become stringy and need straining or turning into jelly. Continually pick these 'fruits' throughout the season, as this promotes further crops.

 ## STORING

Rosellas can be stored in a plastic bag in the refrigerator for a few weeks. Before using rosellas for jam or syrup or drying them to make tea, the green seed pod inside the red calyx should be removed by cutting it out with a small paring knife or by gently pushing an apple corer through the base. If you are making jam don't discard the seed pods, as they contain pectin.

As the first flush of rosellas is usually not enough to make jam, it's useful to know that the fruit can be frozen for up to 6 months. Just wash and dry the fruit, remove the seed pods, and freeze in separate zip-lock bags with as much air removed as possible.

To dry rosellas for tea, discard the seed pods and put the calyxes on a fine-meshed wire rack set on a tray. Place in an oven heated to its lowest temperature with the fan on and the door slightly ajar and dry for a few hours, until dry but still pliable. Leave to cool in the oven then store in a jar, but check after a week to make sure there is no condensation. If there is, dry the rosella in the oven a little longer. Dried rosellas will keep in a cool, dark place for up to 12 months. To use, simply place a rosella in a cup and pour on boiling water. Leave to infuse, and sweeten with honey if desired.

See recipe on page 269

ROSEMARY

☀ GROWING

Who could forget rosemary, the herb of remembrance? It is one of the most useful herbs in cooking, and is also a versatile plant in the garden with different cultivars suitable for walls, hedges or topiary, and even for ground cover. Breeding has also meant that flowers come in white, pink or various shades of blue, but all rosemary has oil-rich leaves perfect for flavouring food.

Rosemary loves a Mediterranean-style climate, but will cope in most climates other than very humid or very cold. It requires great drainage, a sunny position, and an annual dose of lime or dolomite to help sweeten the soil. Prune your plants back after flowering by about 15 cm (6 in).

🦅 HARVESTING

The length of rosemary to cut depends upon your use, with longer sections perfect for skewers and shorter snippets fine for your roast or when you want to strip the leaves from the stem. You can of course use your annual prunings in the kitchen – a good method for collecting these is to place a sheet on the ground and then gather up all the pieces when you are finished pruning.

≡ STORING

You can store fresh rosemary in a plastic bag in the refrigerator for up to 1 week. **To freeze rosemary**, process the leaves with a little oil to make a simple pesto without nuts. Freeze in ice-cube trays, transferring to zip-lock bags when frozen, and store for up to 3 months.

To dry rosemary, wash and remove any browned leaves. Longer stems can be tied in bunches and hung upside down in a warm, dry place away from direct sunlight for 2 weeks. If you're worried about dust, cut some slits in a paper bag and tie this over your bunch. Once crisp, strip off the leaves over baking paper, crumble if desired, and tip into a jar. Store in a cool, dark place for up to 12 months.

To dry shorter stems, strip off the leaves and spread over a tray lined with baking paper. Dry for a few hours in an oven heated to its lowest temperature with the fan on and the door slightly ajar.

To make rosemary salt, use the same method as for oven-drying leaves, but instead scatter them on top of a layer of rock salt. Once dry and cool, blitz for a few moments in a food processor to break up the salt into random flakes with the rosemary blended through. Put into a jar with a plastic-lined lid (salt is corrosive to metal) and store in a cool, dark place for up to 12 months. Use it as a rub for lamb or sprinkle on potatoes or tomatoes for roasting.

See recipe on page 275

SAGE

 ## GROWING

Sage is a pretty grey-leafed plant with purple flowers in summer that the bees adore, and which are also edible. There are a few interesting variegated forms, but for the kitchen, plain sage is far superior with its aromatic and medicinal qualities.

Sage loves an open sunny position. It dislikes humidity and needs protection from frost, and is very fussy about drainage – requiring sandy or friable soil that doesn't hold onto dampness – though it also needs regular water. Lime or dolomite to sweeten the soil and raise the pH also helps with sage success. Sage can be grown from seed or cuttings, in the garden or in pots. Trim it back lightly after flowering to encourage new growth. Each sage plant should live 3 years or so.

 ## HARVESTING

Pick the newer, lighter green sage leaves for immediate use in cooking. They can simply be pinched off with your fingertips.

In late autumn, sage should be trimmed back to about 15 cm (6 in) off the ground. You can use the trimmings in the kitchen – a good method for collecting these is to place a sheet on the ground and then gather up all the pieces when you are finished pruning.

STORING

Sage is best picked from the garden as needed, as it blackens quickly if stored in the refrigerator.

To dry sage, wash and remove any dead or browned leaves. Gather stems together and tie loosely with string or use a rubber band. Make sure you don't overcrowd the bunch or tie it too tightly, as poor air circulation can lead to mould. Hang the bunch upside down in a warm, dry place away from direct sunlight (such as a verandah or porch) for 2 weeks. If you're worried about dust, cut some slits in a brown paper bag and tie this over your bunch before you hang it. The holes will allow airflow. Once crisp and dry, remove the leaves from the stems over a piece of baking paper, crumble if desired, and tip into a jar. Store in a cool, dark place for up to 12 months.

Another method for drying is to strip the leaves from the stems and spread across a tray lined with baking paper, and dry for a few hours in an oven heated to its lowest temperature with the fan on and the door slightly ajar.

See recipe on page 243

TARRAGON

GROWING

Tarragon grows to about 60 cm (2 ft) tall, dying back each winter to a permanent rootstock before reshooting in spring. It is an attractive addition to the garden as each summer the plant is smothered in small yellow daisy-like flowers. Tarragon likes full sun and will tolerate cold climates. However, it can rot if the soil doesn't drain over winter, so if this is a potential problem in your garden try growing it in a pot instead.

HARVESTING

For using tarragon fresh, pick new growth that's light green in colour. For freezing, older darker leaves are preferable. You can also cut off longer stems for drying, but only remove a third of the plant's branches at a time, cutting them off a few centimetres (1 in) from the base. Cut after any dew has dried from the leaves.

STORING

Wrap fresh tarragon in damp paper towel and place inside a plastic bag, storing in the refrigerator for up to 1 week.

To freeze tarragon, follow the directions for coriander (cilantro) on page 118.

To dry tarragon, follow the directions for sage on page 152.

To make tarragon salt, put a layer of rock salt on a tray lined with baking paper. Strip tarragon leaves from their stems and scatter them on top of the salt. Dry for a few hours in an oven heated to its lowest temperature with the fan on and the door slightly ajar. Once dry and cool, blitz for a few moments in a food processor to break up the salt into random flakes with the tarragon blended through. Put into a jar with a plastic-lined lid (salt is corrosive to metal) and store in a cool, dark place for up to 12 months. Use it as a rub for chicken, sprinkle onto fish before baking, or add to vinaigrettes.

To make tarragon vinegar, simply steep a generous handful of washed and dried tarragon sprigs in a jar filled with white-wine vinegar for a few weeks. Strain into a sterilised bottle, seal and store in a cool, dark place for up to 12 months.

See recipes on pages 197, 258 and 329

THYME

GROWING

Thyme, be it lemon, orange or pizza-flavoured, is a worthwhile addition to any garden as it is so pretty – and lovely to brush past and smell. The perennial with edible flowers does well in pots or in the ground. It grows about 20 cm (8 in) tall at best, with some ornamental types growing even lower to the ground as ground covers. To grow thyme well you need to provide good drainage, plenty of sunshine and an annual dressing of lime. It is drought-tolerant once established and will also cope with frost. Common thyme is the most useful variety in the kitchen.

HARVESTING

The flavour of thyme leaves is best before the plant flowers – although of course you can also pick sprigs while flowering and enjoy the flowers too. Harvest in the early morning, and scissors are ideal as they cut cleanly.

Regular trimming means that your stems never become too tough, and it also encourages bushy regrowth.

STORING

To keep thyme fresh, wrap it in damp paper towel, place inside a plastic bag and store in the refrigerator for up to 1 week.

Whole washed and dried sprigs can also be frozen in zip-lock bags with as much air removed as possible, for up to 1 month.

To dry thyme, follow the directions for sage on page 152.

See recipes on pages 162 and 262

SYRUPS AND DRINKS

PASSIONFRUIT AND LEMON-THYME SYRUP

Makes 500 ml (17 fl oz/2 cups)

230 g (8 oz/1 cup) caster
(superfine) sugar
375 ml (12½ fl oz/1½ cups)
water
250 ml (8½ fl oz/1 cup)
passionfruit pulp (about
10 passionfruit)
3 lemon-thyme sprigs

1. Combine the ingredients except the lemon-thyme in a saucepan and place over low heat, stirring until the sugar dissolves. Increase the heat to medium and cook for 10–15 minutes, until syrupy.

2. Pour the hot syrup into warm sterilised jars or bottles. Add the lemon-thyme sprigs and seal immediately. Store in a cool, dark place for up to 12 months. Refrigerate after opening.

COOK'S NOTE

This recipe can be made without lemon-thyme if desired. You can also strain the syrup before bottling to remove the passionfruit seeds (and sprigs of lemon-thyme) for a smooth syrup.

PINEAPPLE, LIME AND MINT SYRUP

Makes 750 ml (25 fl oz/3 cups)

1 kg (2 lb 3 oz) pineapple, peeled, cored and chopped
230 g (8 oz/1 cup) caster (superfine) sugar
250 ml (8½ fl oz/1 cup) water
juice of 2 limes
5 g (¼ oz/¼ cup) mint leaves, torn

1. Put the pineapple in a blender and blend until smooth, then strain into a saucepan. (Alternatively, put the pineapple through a juicer.)

2. Add the remaining ingredients and place over low heat, stirring until the sugar dissolves. Increase the heat to medium and cook, stirring occasionally, for 10–20 minutes, until syrupy.

3. Pour the hot syrup into warm sterilised jars or bottles and seal immediately. Store in a cool, dark place for up to 3 months. Refrigerate after opening.

COOK'S NOTE

Syrups are thicker than cordials – they're delicious on top of ice-cream or yoghurt, blended into smoothies, or swirled through cake or muffin batters.

GREEN-ORANGE SYRUP

Makes 750 ml (25 fl oz/3 cups)

1. Combine the sugar and water in a saucepan and stir over low heat until the sugar dissolves. Add the star anise and increase the heat to medium. Cook for 10 minutes, or until syrupy.

2. Meanwhile, use a zester to remove the rind from the oranges in long strands. (Alternatively, cut off the rind in thin strips with as little white pith as possible and julienne them.) Put into warm sterilised jars or bottles.

3. Pour the hot syrup over the orange zest and seal the jars or bottles immediately. Store in a cool, dark place for up to 12 months. Refrigerate after opening.

COOK'S NOTE

If you have thinned the oranges on your tree, you don't have to just discard the green oranges. While their juice has not yet developed, their zest can be used in this syrup. Use it in an Asian-style dressing to spoon over oysters, add vinegar and oil for a fantastic salad dressing, or simply spoon it over ice-cream along with some of the zest. The zest can also be used in cakes.

460 g (1 lb/2 cups) caster (superfine) sugar
500 ml (17 fl oz/2 cups) water
2 star anise
8 green oranges

RASPBERRY AND APPLE CORDIAL

Makes 2 litres (68 fl oz/8 cups)

1. Combine the raspberries, apples and water in a large saucepan and bring to the boil over high heat. Reduce the heat to medium and cook for 15–20 minutes, until the apple is soft.

2. Strain the liquid through a colander set over a large bowl or saucepan. Discard the solids, then strain the liquid through muslin (cheesecloth) into a measuring jug. Measure the liquid and calculate the quantity of sugar required based on 1 cup of sugar to every 1 cup of liquid.

3. Return the raspberry and apple liquid to the saucepan and add the sugar. Place over low heat, stirring until the sugar dissolves, then increase the heat to medium and cook for 10 minutes. Remove from the heat and stir in the tartaric acid.

4. Pour the hot cordial into warm sterilised bottles and seal immediately. Store in a cool, dark place for up to 12 months. Refrigerate after opening.

1 kg (2 lb 3 oz) raspberries
500 g (1 lb 2 oz) apples, quartered (cores left in)
2 litres (68 fl oz/8 cups) water
caster (superfine) sugar
1 tablespoon tartaric acid

ELDERFLOWER CORDIAL

Makes 750 ml (25 fl oz/3 cups)

690 g (1½ lb/3 cups) caster
  (superfine) sugar
500 ml (17 fl oz/2 cups) water
1 lemon, cut into eighths
20 elderflower heads
1 tablespoon tartaric acid

1. Combine the sugar and water in a saucepan and place over low heat, stirring until the sugar dissolves. Add the lemon pieces and elderflower heads and increase the heat. Boil for 10 minutes.

2. Strain the liquid through a fine-mesh sieve and discard the solids. Return the liquid to the clean saucepan.

3. Return the liquid to the boil, then immediately remove from the heat and stir through the tartaric acid.

4. Pour the hot cordial into warm sterilised bottles and seal immediately. Store in a cool, dark place for up to 12 months. Refrigerate after opening.

COOK'S NOTE

The flavour of elderflower is like nothing else – citrus comes to mind when you first taste it, then vanilla, and there's a slightly spicy aftertaste. If you miss the time to pick the flower heads, hold off until the berries form and ripen and make **elderberry cordial** *instead. Use 500 g (1 lb 2 oz) of elderberries in place of the elderflowers in this recipe, and omit the lemon.*

Elderflower
Cordial

Elderberry
Cordial

LEMON CORDIAL

Makes 875 ml (30 fl oz/3½ cups)

690 g (1½ lb/3 cups) caster
   (superfine) sugar
500 ml (17 fl oz/2 cups) water
juice of 4 lemons
1 tablespoon tartaric acid

1. Combine the sugar and water in a saucepan and place over low heat, stirring until the sugar dissolves. Increase the heat and boil for 10 minutes. Add the lemon juice and boil for another 5 minutes, until syrupy. Remove from the heat and stir through the tartaric acid.

2. Pour the hot cordial into warm sterilised bottles and seal immediately. Store in a cool, dark place for up to 12 months. Refrigerate after opening.

COOK'S NOTE

*For a **quick and easy lemonade**, combine 4 chopped lemons, 460 g (1 lb/2 cups) of caster (superfine) sugar and 375 ml (12½ fl oz/1½ cups) of water in a blender and blend until smooth. Strain the mixture through muslin (cheesecloth) into a bottle and store in the refrigerator for up to 1 week. Mix with mineral or soda water (club soda) to make lemonade. Makes 750 ml (25 fl oz/3 cups) of syrup.*

FRESH APPLE CIDER

Use a mixture of 3 or more apple varieties such as royal gala, pink lady and golden delicious. This helps give a balanced flavour. Put the washed whole apples through a clean fruit press, collecting the juice in a clean bucket or tub. Strain through muslin (cheesecloth) into bottles. You can enjoy the cider immediately or store in the refrigerator for up to 1 week, in which case your bottles should be sterilised.

COOK'S NOTE

There is some debate over the difference between apple juice and fresh apple cider, but the answer is simple: apple juice is made from pressed apples, which is then heated or pasteurised and bottled; while fresh apple cider is juice that is bottled raw.

This makes cider more perishable and it needs to be refrigerated, whereas juice has a longer shelf life.

APPLE JUICE

Unlike cider, it is not important to use a variety of apples, but feel free to experiment if you have several varieties of apples on hand. Put the washed whole apples through a juicer or fruit press, then pour the juice into a saucepan. Bring to the boil, then strain through muslin (cheesecloth) into warm sterilised bottles and seal immediately. Store in a cool, dark place for up to 3 months. Refrigerate after opening.

BLACKBERRY GIN

Makes 750 ml (25 fl oz/3 cups)

500 g (1 lb 2 oz) blackberries
750 ml (25 fl oz/3 cups) gin
115 g (4 oz/½ cup) caster
  (superfine) sugar
125 ml (4 fl oz/½ cup) water

1. Divide the blackberries between 2 x 750 ml (25 fl oz) sterilised bottles. Top up with the gin. Seal and store in a cool, dark place. Shake the bottles every second day for 1 week, then leave for 1–3 months to mature.

2. To finish the gin, strain the gin through muslin (cheesecloth) and discard the blackberries. Return the gin to the bottles. Combine the sugar and water in a small saucepan and place over low heat, stirring until the sugar dissolves. Leave to cool before adding to the gin a little at a time, tasting after each addition to ensure the gin does not become too sweet. When the flavour is to your liking, seal the bottles again and store for up to 12 months.

COOK'S NOTE

Mulberries work equally well in this easy recipe.

PINEAPPLE VODKA

Makes 1.5 litres (50 fl oz/6 cups)

400 g (14 oz) peeled, cored
and chopped pineapple
(about ½ medium
pineapple)
1 litre (34 fl oz/4 cups) vodka
115 g (4 oz/½ cup) caster
(superfine) sugar
125 ml (4 fl oz/½ cup) water

1. Put the pineapple in a large jar or wide-necked bottle
    (approximately 1.5 litres/50 fl oz/6 cups in capacity). Cover
    with the vodka. Seal and store in a cool, dark place for
    1 week.

2. To finish the vodka, combine the sugar and water in a small
    saucepan and place over low heat, stirring until the sugar
    dissolves. Leave to cool, then add to the vodka, swirling
    to combine.

3. Blend the vodka mixture in batches until smooth
    (alternatively, use a hand-held blender directly in the jar).
    Strain through muslin (cheesecloth) into sterilised bottles.
    Store in the refrigerator for up to 1 month.

SORBETS, SHERBETS AND GRANITAS

MELON AND LEMONGRASS GRANITA

Makes 1 litre (34 fl oz/4 cups)

2 lemongrass stalks
230 g (8 oz/1 cup) caster
  (superfine) sugar
250 ml (8½ fl oz/1 cup) water
700 g (1 lb 9 oz) diced
  rockmelon (about 1 small
  rockmelon)

1. Use the back of a large knife or a mallet to bruise the lemongrass stalks. Tie each stalk in a loose knot.

2. Heat the sugar and water in a small saucepan over low heat, stirring until the sugar dissolves. Add the lemongrass and increase the heat to high. Boil for 5 minutes, or until syrupy, then set aside to cool.

3. Put the rockmelon in a food processor and blend until smooth. Strain in the syrup and blend until combined.

4. Pour the melon mixture into a wide metal tray and freeze for 1 hour, until beginning to set around the edges. Use a fork to rake the frozen edges of the granita into the centre, and break up large pieces of ice to a slushy texture. Freeze for another hour, then repeat. Do this 3–4 times until the granita is firm. While this granita is best enjoyed soon after it is made, it can be stored in the freezer for up to 2 weeks. If storing, put the mixture into an airtight container after the last raking.

COOK'S NOTE

Sorbets, granitas and sherbets are some of the most refreshing things you can make in summer. To demystify their different names – a sorbet is generally based on a fruit purée combined with sugar syrup, sometimes including egg whites, churned to a smooth texture; granita has the same fruit and sugar basis but is allowed to become granular and icy as it freezes; and sherbets, while not as rich as ice-cream, are creamier than sorbets with the addition of buttermilk, yoghurt or milk.

BASIL AND YOGHURT SHERBET

Makes 1.2 litres (41 fl oz/4¾ cups)

230 g (8 oz/1 cup) caster
(superfine) sugar
250 ml (8½ fl oz/1 cup) water
100 g (3½ oz/2 cups) basil
leaves
1 kg (2 lb 3 oz/4 cups)
Greek-style yoghurt

1. Heat the sugar and water in a small saucepan over low heat, stirring until the sugar dissolves. Increase the heat to high and boil for 5 minutes, or until syrupy. Remove from the heat, stir in the basil and leave to cool.

2. Strain the syrup into a large bowl, pressing down on the basil leaves to extract their flavour. Mix the yoghurt into the syrup.

3. Pour the yoghurt mixture into a wide metal tray and freeze for 3–4 hours, until just firm.

4. Remove the sherbet from the freezer and cut into pieces while still in the tray. Scoop the pieces into a food processor and blend until smooth (do this in batches if necessary), then return the mixture to the tray. Freeze overnight until firm. This sherbet can be stored in the freezer for up to 1 month – if storing, put the mixture into an airtight container after blending. It is delicious served with strawberries.

COOK'S NOTE

If you have an ice-cream machine, then by all means use it for any of these sorbet and sherbet recipes – just churn according to the manufacturer's instructions. Note that the sorbets and sherbets will actually store in the freezer for about 3 months, although their texture gradually becomes more and more icy.

MANGO AND LIME SHERBET

Makes 750 ml (25 fl oz/3 cups)

2 mangoes, flesh chopped
250 ml (8½ fl oz/1 cup)
  buttermilk
30 g (1 oz/¼ cup) icing
  (confectioners') sugar
2 tablespoons lime juice

1. Purée the mango in a food processor. Add the remaining ingredients and blend until combined. Pour the mixture into a wide metal tray and freeze for 3 hours.

2. Scrape the mixture back into the food processor and blend, then return to the tray and freeze for a further 4 hours, until firm. This sherbet can be stored in the freezer for up to 1 month – if storing, put the mixture into an airtight container after blending.

RHUBARB AND COCONUT SHERBET

Makes 750 ml (25 fl oz/3 cups)

1. Combine the rhubarb, sugar and water in a saucepan. Cover and simmer for 5 minutes, or until the rhubarb is soft and the liquid is syrupy. Leave to cool.

2. Blend the rhubarb with a hand-held blender until smooth. Add the yoghurt and stir to combine.

3. Pour the mixture into a wide metal tray and freeze for 3–4 hours, until just firm.

4. Remove the sherbet from the freezer and cut into pieces while still in the tray. Scoop the pieces into a food processor and blend until smooth (do this in batches if necessary), then return the mixture to the tray. Freeze overnight. This sherbet can be stored in the freezer for up to 1 month – if storing, put the mixture into an airtight container after blending.

300 g (10½ oz) rhubarb, chopped
230 g (8 oz/1 cup) caster (superfine) sugar
60 ml (2 fl oz/¼ cup) water
500 g (1 lb 2 oz/2 cups) coconut yoghurt

GUAVA AND LIME SORBET

Makes 750 ml (25 fl oz/3 cups)

1 kg (2 lb 3 oz) pink-
fleshed apple guava,
chopped (including skin)
230 g (8 oz/1 cup) caster
(superfine) sugar
1 lime, zested and juiced

1. Purée the guava in a blender or food processor. Strain through a fine-mesh sieve into a saucepan, discarding the pulp. This should give you about 750 ml (25 fl oz/3 cups) of juice.

2. Add the sugar and lime juice and stir over low heat until the sugar dissolves. Increase the heat to medium and cook for 5 minutes, or until syrupy. Remove from the heat and stir through the lime zest. Set aside to cool.

3. Pour the mixture into a wide metal tray and freeze for 3–4 hours, until just firm.

4. Remove the sorbet from the freezer and cut into pieces while still in the tray. Scoop the pieces into a food processor and blend until smooth (do this in batches if necessary), then return the mixture to the tray. Freeze for a further 3 hours, until firm. This sorbet can be stored in the freezer for up to 1 month – if storing, put the mixture into an airtight container after blending.

SPICE PASTES AND PESTOS

HARISSA
190

GREEN CURRY PASTE
192

TIKKA MASALA PASTE
194

CHERMOULA
195

ROASTED TOMATO PESTO
197

MIXED HERB PESTO
198

KALE AND PEANUT PESTO
199

BROCCOLI AND CHILLI PESTO
200

ROCKET, BASIL AND
MACADAMIA NUT PESTO
202

PEA AND MINT PESTO
203

MUSHROOM DUXELLES
204

HARISSA

Makes 500 ml (17 fl oz/2 cups)

200 g (7 oz) red chillies
  (a mixture of varieties
  and heat as desired)
3 red capsicums
  (bell peppers)
1 small garlic bulb
1 teaspoon cumin seeds
1 teaspoon coriander seeds
1 teaspoon fennel seeds
60 ml (2 fl oz/¼ cup)
  white-wine vinegar
60 ml (2 fl oz/¼ cup)
  extra-virgin olive oil,
  plus extra for the jar

1. Preheat the oven to 200°C/180°C fan-forced (400°F/350°F).
    Put the whole chillies, capsicums and garlic on a large
    tray (lined with baking paper if desired) and bake for
    20 minutes, until the skins are lightly charred. Transfer
    the chillies and capsicums to a bowl, cover with plastic
    wrap and leave to cool (the steam helps loosen their skins).

2. Toast the cumin, coriander and fennel seeds in a dry frying
    pan for 1–2 minutes, until fragrant. Leave to cool.

3. Peel the chillies and capsicums and remove their seeds.
    Put the flesh into a food processor. Squeeze the garlic
    cloves from their skins and add to the processor, followed
    by the toasted spices. Process until finely chopped. Add
    the vinegar and oil and process to a paste.

4. Spoon into a sterilised jar and cover with a layer of oil.
    Store in the refrigerator for up to 2 months.

COOK'S NOTE

*Harissa is a fantastic base for marinades and stir-fries.
You can use any fresh, ripe chillies you have on hand, or
a mix of varieties for different flavours and heat. You can
even used dried chillies – just soak them until soft instead
of roasting them.*

GREEN CURRY PASTE

Makes 375 ml (12½ fl oz/1½ cups)

2 teaspoons coriander seeds

2 teaspoons cumin seeds

2 teaspoons white
  peppercorns

1 onion, roughly chopped

4 cm (1½ in) piece of ginger,
  roughly chopped

4 garlic cloves, roughly
  chopped

10 long green chillies, seeded
  if desired, roughly chopped

2 lemongrass stalks,
  white part only, sliced

6 coriander (cilantro) roots
  with stems and leaves
  attached, well washed
  and chopped

4 kaffir lime leaves, shredded

2 tablespoons vegetable oil

1. Toast the coriander seeds, cumin seeds and peppercorns
   in a dry frying pan for 1–2 minutes, until fragrant.

2. Combine the remaining ingredients with the spices in a
   food processor. Process to a smooth paste.

3. Spoon into a jar and store in the refrigerator for up to
   1 week. Alternatively, spoon into an ice-cube tray and
   freeze overnight, then transfer the cubes to a zip-lock
   bag and store in the freezer for up to 3 months. When
   ready to use, place the required number of cubes in
   a bowl and defrost in the refrigerator.

COOK'S NOTE

*Using long green chillies rather than small fiery ones gives
you a milder curry paste. However, if you're feeling brave, turn
up the heat by using some or all small, hot green chillies. This
recipe can also be used to make red curry paste – simply use
red chillies instead of green.*

TIKKA MASALA PASTE

Makes 750 ml (25 fl oz/3 cups)

4 tomatoes
1 tablespoon coriander seeds
1 tablespoon cumin seeds
1 teaspoon cardamom seeds,
  roughly ground
1 teaspoon yellow mustard
  seeds
4 onions, roughly chopped
6 garlic cloves, roughly
  chopped
4 cm (1½ in) piece of ginger,
  roughly chopped
6 long red chillies, seeded
  and roughly chopped

1. Use a small, sharp knife to cut a shallow cross in the base of each tomato. Drop the tomatoes into a saucepan of simmering water for 15 seconds. Scoop them out with a slotted spoon and drop into a bowl of iced water. When cool enough to handle, peel the tomatoes.

2. Toast the coriander, cumin, cardamom and mustard seeds in a dry frying pan for 1–2 minutes, until fragrant.

3. Combine the tomatoes, spices and remaining ingredients in a food processor. Process to a smooth paste.

4. Spoon into a jar and store in the refrigerator for up to 1 week. Alternatively, spoon into an ice-cube tray and freeze overnight, then transfer the cubes to a zip-lock bag and store in the freezer for up to 3 months. When ready to use, place the required number of cubes in a bowl and defrost in the refrigerator.

COOK'S NOTE

This popular curry paste is mild and versatile, being ideal for chicken, fish or vegetable curries. For a quick chicken curry, fry chopped onion and chicken pieces in a little oil, then add some paste and continue to fry for a few minutes. Pour in coconut milk and simmer away.

CHERMOULA

Makes 250 ml (8½ fl oz/1 cup)

1. Toast the coriander seeds, cumin seeds, peppercorns and chilli flakes in a dry frying pan for 1–2 minutes, until fragrant. Grind the spices using a mortar and pestle.

2. Put the remaining ingredients in a food processor along with the spices. Process to a smooth paste.

3. Spoon into a jar and store in the refrigerator for up to 1 week. Alternatively, spoon into an ice-cube tray and freeze overnight, then transfer the cubes to a zip-lock bag and store in the freezer for up to 3 months. When ready to use, place the required number of cubes in a bowl and defrost in the refrigerator.

COOK'S NOTE

This herby marinade is traditionally used for fish, although it can be used on a variety of other meats, especially lamb.

2 teaspoons coriander seeds
2 teaspoons cumin seeds
2 teaspoons white
   peppercorns
1 teaspoon chilli flakes
1 onion, roughly chopped
2 garlic cloves, roughly
   chopped
120 g (4 oz/2 cups)
   chopped parsley
100 g (3½ oz/2 cups)
   chopped coriander
   (cilantro)
juice of 1 lemon
60 ml (2 fl oz/¼ cup)
   olive oil

ROASTED TOMATO PESTO

Makes 1 litre (34 fl oz/4 cups)

1. Preheat the oven to 200°C/180°C fan-forced (400°F/350°F). Spread the tomatoes across 2 large trays lined with baking paper. Drizzle with the vinegar and 2 tablespoons of the oil. Scatter over the tarragon and season well. Roast for 45 minutes, until the tomatoes are soft and browned. Set aside to cool.

2. Peel the skins from the tomato pieces (they should be very loose and almost falling off). Use the paper to tip the flesh and juices into a food processor. Add the garlic, parmesan and pine nuts. Process until well chopped, then add the remaining 60 ml (2 fl oz/¼ cup) of oil and process until smooth.

3. Transfer to jars, covering the surface with a little extra oil, and store in the refrigerator for up to 2 weeks. Alternatively, spoon into ice-cube trays and freeze overnight, then transfer the cubes to a zip-lock bag and store in the freezer for up to 3 months. When ready to use, place the required number of cubes in a bowl and defrost in the refrigerator.

COOK'S NOTE

Pesto is a great thing to have on hand for a quick and easy dinner, and there are so many delicious ways of using it. Stir it through hot pasta or potatoes, add it to sour cream for a salad dressing, or use it as a topping for bruschetta. Pesto also freezes well – thawed pesto tastes as good as freshly made, even if the colour may dull slightly.

1.5 kg (3 lb 5 oz) tomatoes, quartered

60 ml (2 fl oz/¼ cup) raspberry or red-wine vinegar

100 ml (3½ fl oz) extra-virgin olive oil, plus extra for the jars

2 tarragon sprigs, leaves stripped from the stems

salt and pepper

1 garlic clove, chopped

100 g (3½ oz/1 cup) grated parmesan

80 g (3 oz/½ cup) pine nuts

MIXED HERB PESTO

Makes 500 ml (17 fl oz/2 cups)

100 g (3½ oz/2 cups)
  basil leaves
80 g (3 oz/2 cups)
  parsley leaves
25 g (1 oz/½ cup)
  snipped chives
60 g (2 oz/½ cup)
  slivered almonds
100 g (3½ oz/1 cup)
  grated parmesan
250 ml (8½ fl oz/1 cup)
  extra-virgin olive oil,
  plus extra for the jars

1. Combine the herbs, almonds and parmesan in a food processor and process until finely chopped. Add the oil and process until smooth.

2. Transfer to jars, covering the surface with a little extra oil, and store in the refrigerator for up to 2 weeks. Alternatively, spoon into ice-cube trays and freeze overnight, then transfer the cubes to a zip-lock bag and store in the freezer for up to 3 months. When ready to use, place the required number of cubes in a bowl and defrost in the refrigerator.

KALE AND PEANUT PESTO

Makes 625 ml (21 fl oz/2½ cups)

1. Put the kale into a heatproof bowl and cover with boiling water. Set aside for 5 minutes, until the kale is wilted, then drain and rinse under cold water. Drain well.

2. Combine the peanuts, garlic and lemon juice in a food processor and process until chopped. Add the kale in batches and continue to process until finely chopped. Add the parmesan and oil and process until smooth.

3. Transfer to jars, covering the surface with a little extra oil, and store in the refrigerator for up to 2 weeks. Alternatively, spoon into ice-cube trays and freeze overnight, then transfer the cubes to a zip-lock bag and store in the freezer for up to 3 months. When ready to use, place the required number of cubes in a bowl and defrost in the refrigerator.

350 g (12 oz) kale (any variety), ends trimmed, chopped
80 g (3 oz/½ cup) roasted peanuts
3 garlic cloves, chopped
juice of 1 lemon
100 g (3½ oz/1 cup) grated parmesan
125 ml (4 fl oz/½ cup) extra-virgin olive oil, plus extra for the jars

BROCCOLI AND CHILLI PESTO

Makes 750 ml (25 fl oz/3 cups)

2 broccoli heads, chopped
2 garlic cloves, chopped
2 long green chillies,
   seeded and chopped
20 g (¾ oz/1 cup)
   mint leaves
100 g (3½ oz/1 cup)
   grated parmesan
50 g (2 oz/⅓ cup)
   roasted cashew nuts
250 ml (8½ fl oz/1 cup)
   extra-virgin olive oil,
   plus extra for the jars

1. Cook the broccoli in a large saucepan of boiling water for 2–3 minutes. (Alternatively, put the broccoli in a heatproof bowl, add a splash of water, then cover and microwave on high for 3 minutes.) Transfer the cooked broccoli to a bowl of iced water to cool, then drain.

2. Combine the broccoli, garlic, chilli, mint, parmesan and cashew nuts in a food processor. Process until finely chopped, then add the oil and process until smooth.

3. Transfer to jars, covering the surface with a little extra oil, and store in the refrigerator for up to 2 weeks. Alternatively, spoon into ice-cube trays and freeze overnight, then transfer the cubes to a zip-lock bag and store in the freezer for up to 3 months. When ready to use, place the required number of cubes in a bowl and defrost in the refrigerator.

ROCKET, BASIL AND MACADAMIA NUT PESTO

Makes 500 ml (17 fl oz/2 cups)

150 g (5 oz) rocket (arugula)
50 g (2 oz/1 cup) basil leaves
100 g (3½ oz/1 cup)
    grated parmesan
80 g (3 oz/½ cup)
    macadamia nuts
1 garlic clove, chopped
125 ml (4 fl oz/½ cup)
    extra-virgin olive oil,
    plus extra for the jars

1. Combine the rocket, basil, parmesan, macadamia nuts and garlic in a food processor and process until finely chopped. Add the oil and process until smooth.

2. Transfer to jars, covering the surface with a little extra oil, and store in the refrigerator for up to 2 weeks. Alternatively, spoon into ice-cube trays and freeze overnight, then transfer the cubes to a zip-lock bag and store in the freezer for up to 3 months. When ready to use, place the required number of cubes in a bowl and defrost in the refrigerator.

PEA AND MINT PESTO

Makes 750 ml (25 fl oz/3 cups)

1. Heat a third of the oil in a small saucepan over medium heat. Fry the garlic for 30 seconds until fragrant, then add the peas and water and simmer for 4–5 minutes until tender. Set aside to cool completely.

2. Combine the pea mixture, mint, parmesan and pine nuts in a food processor and process until finely chopped. Add the remaining oil and process until smooth.

3. Transfer to jars, covering the surface with a little extra oil, and store in the refrigerator for up to 2 weeks. Alternatively, spoon into ice-cube trays and freeze overnight, then transfer the cubes to a zip-lock bag and store in the freezer for up to 3 months. When ready to use, place the required number of cubes in a bowl and defrost in the refrigerator.

60 ml (2 fl oz/¼ cup)
  extra-virgin olive oil,
  plus extra for the jars
1 garlic clove, chopped
230 g (8 oz/1½ cups) peas,
  fresh or frozen
190 ml (6½ fl oz/¾ cup)
  water
30 g (1 oz/1½ cups)
  mint leaves
75 g (2½ oz/¾ cup)
  grated parmesan
40 g (1½ oz/¼ cup)
  pine nuts, toasted

MUSHROOM DUXELLES

Makes 375 ml (12½ fl oz/1½ cups)

1 tablespoon olive oil

1 onion, finely chopped

100 g (3½ oz) pancetta, finely chopped

2 garlic cloves, finely chopped

250 g (9 oz) button mushrooms, very finely chopped

250 g (9 oz) swiss brown mushrooms, very finely chopped

2 teaspoons dijon mustard

1. Heat the oil in a frying pan over medium heat. Fry the onion for 5 minutes until soft, then add the pancetta and fry for another 3 minutes until browned, stirring regularly. Add the garlic and cook for a further minute until fragrant. Add the mushrooms and cook, stirring occasionally, for 15 minutes, until the mushrooms are soft and dry. Stir through the mustard.

2. Leave to cool, then spoon into a jar or airtight container and store in the refrigerator for up to 1 week, or in the freezer for up to 2 months.

COOK'S NOTE

This flavoursome mushroom paste can be used as a topping for bruschetta, steak or hamburgers, stirred through pasta or gnocchi, or used as a filling for ravioli or omelettes.

FLAVOURED BUTTERS and SALTS

CHIVE BUTTER

208

DILL AND LEMON BUTTER

208

MINT SALT

210

CHILLI SALT

210

TOMATO SALT

210

CHIVE BUTTER

Makes 250 g (9 oz)

250 g (9 oz) butter, softened
20 g (¾ oz/⅓ cup) snipped
   chives

1. Combine the butter and chives in a bowl and stir until well blended. Spoon onto a large piece of baking paper and roll into a log inside the paper. Twist the ends, fold them under and refrigerate for 1 hour, or until firm.

2. Store the log in the refrigerator in its paper wrapping for up to 1 month, or in the freezer for up to 3 months. Cut slices from the refrigerated or frozen log as needed.

DILL AND LEMON BUTTER

Makes 250 g (9 oz)

250 g (9 oz) butter, softened
20 g (¾ oz/⅓ cup)
   chopped dill
grated zest of 2 lemons

1. Combine the butter, dill and lemon zest in a bowl and stir until well blended. Spoon onto a large piece of baking paper and roll into a log inside the paper. Twist the ends, fold them under and refrigerate for 1 hour, or until firm.

2. Store the log in the refrigerator in its paper wrapping for up to 1 month, or in the freezer for up to 3 months. Cut slices from the refrigerated or frozen log as needed.

COOK'S NOTE

You can pan-fry fish, scallops or prawns (shrimp) in herb butter (the dill and lemon butter is particularly good for this); serve it with grilled meat or chicken; or even use it as a base for a white sauce. You can change the flavour with any herb or a combination of several herbs, and adding spices such as Moroccan or cajun spice mix works well too.

MINT SALT

Makes 35 g (1 oz/¼ cup)

35 g (1 oz/¼ cup) sea salt flakes
5 g (¼ oz/¼ cup) mint leaves

1. Put the salt and mint in a small food processor or spice grinder and pulse until combined. This fresh herb salt is best used soon after it is made, but can be stored in an airtight container in a cool, dark place for up to 1 week.

CHILLI SALT

Makes 65 g (2 oz/½ cup)

65 g (2 oz/½ cup) sea salt flakes
5 dried chillies of any variety, seeded if desired

1. Put the salt and chillies in a small food processor and pulse until the chillies are well chopped. You can also add lemon zest for a citrus note. Store in an airtight container in a cool, dark place for up to 6 months.

TOMATO SALT

Makes 65 g (2 oz/½ cup)

skins from 5 tomatoes
65 g (2 oz/½ cup) sea salt flakes

1. Preheat the oven to its lowest temperature. Line a tray with baking paper and lay the tomato skins on top. Dry in the oven for about 2 hours, until crisp. Leave to cool, then use your hands to crush the skins into a bowl. Add the salt and toss to combine. Store in an airtight container in a cool, dark place for up to 6 months.

COOK'S NOTE

Only limited by your imagination and tastebuds, flavoured salts can become a cook's best friend. Use them in place of normal salt in rubs, salad dressings, casseroles and on roast vegetables. Most flavourings need to be dried first, which can be done in the oven or a dehydrator. Try mushrooms, citrus peel, herbs, edible flowers and dried fruit. A basic guide is 1 teaspoon of dried flavourings to 35 g (1 oz/¼ cup) of the best sea salt flakes you can afford. Salts made with dried flavourings last a good while.

VINEGARS

HOMEMADE VINEGAR

Making vinegar from scratch is simple, it just takes time and patience!

There are two basic stages in making vinegar – and it can be made from almost any liquid. In the first fermentation yeasts convert sugar to alcohol. In the second stage the alcohol is converted to acetic acid, or vinegar.

While you can start from the very beginning and make your own alcoholic liquid, it is easier to take a shortcut and start at the second stage, using alcohol, water and a vinegar starter or 'mother' to get the process going.

You can purchase the starter, or simply use what you have in the pantry, as starter can be found in the sediment of any wine vinegar or cider vinegar. This is the process I use.

To get started, pour off the vinegar from any preservative-free bottle of vinegar you have in the cupboard, stopping once you reach the sediment at the bottom of the bottle. Pour the sediment into a large glass bottle. Fill the bottle with equal parts of pure water and either red wine, white wine or apple cider (alcoholic), depending on the flavour you desire. The better the quality of wine or cider you use, the better the vinegar will be. You can try any variety of wine – among the reds I love using cabernet sauvignon. Cover the bottle opening with a double layer of muslin (cheesecloth) and secure with a rubber band (leave the bottle's lid off). Store in a cool, dark place for 3 months.

Commercially made vinegar is tested for readiness in two ways – the pH, and the acidity concentration percentage. Testing for acidity concentration requires a special test kit that is available from brewing suppliers. However, testing for pH alone is a good general indicator of readiness, and is much easier for the home vinegar-maker. You can use pH strips, which are available from pool shops, hardware stores and chemists. The colour of the strip will tell you how acidic the vinegar is – you are looking for a pH between 3 and 5. (The vinegar starts out alkaline with a high pH and gradually moves down, with 3 being more acidic.)

From 3 months to 6 months you should start testing your vinegar with the pH strips, and taste it at the same time to check the flavour. Once it is getting close to the right pH range, or is in the right range but you would prefer it a little more acidic, you should test the vinegar weekly. When you are happy with the vinegar, strain it through a piece of muslin (cheesecloth) into sterilised bottles and seal. It should keep for up to 2 years in a cool, dark place.

Vinegar made and tested this way is perfectly suitable for salad dressings or seasoning, but is not recommended for pickling due to the uncertainty of the acidity concentration.

HERB VINEGAR

handful of your herb of
choice (such as tarragon,
chives, rosemary or thyme)
white-wine vinegar

1. Wash the herb and pat dry with paper towel or a clean
   tea towel. Cut if necessary, and put into a jar. Cover with
   white-wine vinegar. Seal and stand at room temperature
   for 2–3 weeks, turning or shaking the jar daily.

2. Strain the vinegar, pour into a sterilised bottle, and seal.
   Store in a cool, dark place for up to 12 months.

CHILLI VINEGAR

fresh or dried chillies
of any variety
white vinegar

1. Drop whole or split chillies into a warm sterilised bottle.
   Heat white vinegar until boiling, then pour into the bottle
   and seal. Store in a cool, dark place for 6 weeks before
   using, and use within 12 months.

TOMATO VINEGAR

Makes 1 litre (34 fl oz/4 cups)

500 g (1 lb 2 oz) tomatoes,
chopped
1 litre (34 fl oz/4 cups) white
vinegar
115 g (4 oz/½ cup) caster
(superfine) sugar

1. Put the tomatoes in a large glass container with a lid. Add
   the vinegar and mix well. Cover with the lid and set aside
   for 5 days, stirring daily.

2. Strain through muslin (cheesecloth) into a saucepan. Add the
   sugar and stir over low heat until dissolved. Bring to the boil,
   then pour into warm sterilised bottles and seal. Store in a
   cool, dark place for up to 12 months. The vinegar has a
   subtle tomato taste and is great in salads.

COOK'S NOTE

Vinegar can be flavoured with spices, herbs, fruit and even vegetables. Use either red- or white-wine vinegar, or plain white vinegar if you prefer. I often use a commercially made straight white vinegar because the end product is more reflective of the flavour you are trying to impart. The process is simple: you just steep the ingredient in the vinegar for several days or up to a couple of weeks before straining. If you have used a fruit or vegetable, then you also need to heat the vinegar to boiling point after steeping. Pour into sterilised bottles and store the flavoured vinegar in a cool, dark place for up to 12 months.

RASPBERRY VINEGAR

Makes 500 ml (17 fl oz/2 cups)

125 g (4 oz/1 cup)
  raspberries
500 ml (17 fl oz/2 cups)
  white vinegar
115 g (4 oz/½ cup) caster
  (superfine) sugar

1. Lightly mash the raspberries in a glass container with a lid.
   Add the vinegar and mix well. Cover with the lid and set
   aside for 5 days, stirring daily.

2. Strain the vinegar through muslin (cheesecloth) into a
   saucepan. Add the sugar and stir over low heat until
   dissolved. Bring to the boil, then remove from the heat, pour
   into a warm sterilised bottle and seal immediately. Store in
   a cool, dark place for up to 12 months. Raspberry vinegar
   can be used in so many ways, such as to season ratatouille,
   bolognese and lentils, and also in salad dressings.

SAUCES AND SALSAS

TOMATO KETCHUP
222

SPICY PLUM SAUCE
224

APPLE AND FENNEL SAUCE
225

SMOKY BARBECUE SAUCE
226

SWEET CHILLI SAUCE
228

CHILLI DIPPING SAUCE
230

HORSERADISH CREAM
231

PINEAPPLE AND
JALAPEÑO SALSA
232

MANGO AND
COCONUT SALSA
234

PAPAYA, LIME
AND CHILLI SALSA
235

CHARGRILLED CORN
AND BEAN SALSA
236

TOMATO KETCHUP

Makes 750 ml (25 fl oz/3 cups)

2 kg (4 lb 6 oz) ripe
   tomatoes, quartered
3 onions, chopped
2 garlic cloves, chopped
2 teaspoons salt
pepper
115 g (4 oz/½ cup) caster
   (superfine) sugar
60 ml (2 fl oz/¼ cup)
   red-wine vinegar

1. Combine the tomatoes, onion and garlic in a food
   processor and process until the tomato is roughly
   chopped (do this in batches if necessary).

2. Transfer to a large saucepan and add the salt and a
   grinding of pepper. Bring to the boil then reduce the
   heat to low, cover with a lid and simmer for 45 minutes,
   stirring occasionally.

3. Pass the tomato mixture through a food mill (or press
   through a sieve, pushing down to extract as much liquid
   as possible). Discard the solids.

4. Return the strained mixture to the clean saucepan. Add the
   sugar and vinegar and bring to the boil, then reduce the
   heat to low and simmer for 20–30 minutes with the lid off,
   stirring regularly, until thickened slightly. Taste for seasoning,
   adding more salt or sugar if desired.

5. Pour the hot sauce into warm sterilised bottles or jars
   and seal immediately. Store in a cool, dark place for up
   to 12 months. Refrigerate after opening.

SPICY PLUM SAUCE

Makes 2 litres (68 fl oz/8 cups)

1.5 kg (3 lb 5 oz) plums
  of any variety, stoned
  and chopped
1 onion, chopped
2 garlic cloves, chopped
2 cm (¾ in) piece of ginger,
  chopped
2 long red chillies, seeded
  if desired, chopped
2 teaspoons sichuan
  peppercorns, ground
2 teaspoons Chinese
  five-spice
2 teaspoons ground cumin
1 teaspoon salt
185 g (6½ oz/1 cup)
  soft brown sugar
375 ml (12½ fl oz/1½ cups)
  red-wine vinegar
250 ml (8½ fl oz/1 cup) water
80 ml (2½ fl oz/⅓ cup)
  tamari

1. Combine all the ingredients in a large heavy-based
    saucepan and bring to the boil. Reduce the heat to low
    and simmer, covered, for 20 minutes, or until the plums
    have completely collapsed.

2. Allow to cool slightly before puréeing with a hand-
    held blender. Strain into another saucepan. Simmer
    for 15–20 minutes, until the sauce has thickened slightly.

3. Pour the hot sauce into warm sterilised bottles or jars
    and seal immediately. Store in a cool, dark place for up
    to 12 months. Refrigerate after opening.

APPLE AND FENNEL SAUCE

Makes 500 ml (17 fl oz/2 cups)

1. Combine all the ingredients in a large saucepan and bring to the boil. Reduce the heat to low and simmer, covered, for 15–20 minutes, until the apples are soft. Remove from the heat.

2. Purée the sauce with a hand-held blender. Return to a simmer and cook for another 5 minutes, or until thickened slightly.

3. Ladle the hot sauce into warm sterilised jars and seal immediately. Store in a cool, dark place for up to 3 months. If you heat-process the jars (see page 12), you can extend the shelf life to 12 months. Refrigerate after opening.

1 kg (2 lb 3 oz) mixed apples, peeled, cored and chopped

115 g (4 oz/½ cup) caster (superfine) sugar

1 tablespoon fennel seeds, toasted

125 ml (4 fl oz/½ cup) water

SMOKY BARBECUE SAUCE

Makes 750 ml (25 fl oz/3 cups)

1 kg (2 lb 3 oz) ripe tomatoes
1 onion, chopped
2 garlic cloves, chopped
2 teaspoons mustard powder
2 tablespoons smoked
  paprika
1 teaspoon salt
95 g (3½ oz/½ cup)
  soft brown sugar
60 ml (2 fl oz/¼ cup)
  worcestershire sauce

1. Boil the tomatoes in a large saucepan of salted water for 3–5 minutes, until their skins split and they soften slightly. Scoop from the water and set aside to cool before peeling the tomatoes.

2. Combine the peeled tomatoes, onion, garlic, mustard powder, paprika and salt in a food processor and process until smooth. Strain through a fine-mesh sieve into a saucepan, pressing through as much liquid as possible. Discard the solids. Add the sugar and worcestershire sauce to the pan and bring to the boil, then reduce the heat and simmer for 20 minutes, or until thickened.

3. Pour the hot sauce into warm sterilised bottles or jars and seal immediately. Store in a cool, dark place for up to 12 months. Refrigerate after opening.

SWEET CHILLI SAUCE

Makes 500 ml (17 fl oz/2 cups)

250 g (9 oz) long red chillies,
  seeded if desired, roughly
  chopped
6 red bird's eye chillies,
  seeded if desired, roughly
  chopped
5 garlic cloves, roughly
  chopped
460 g (1 lb/2 cups) caster
  (superfine) sugar
500 ml (17 fl oz/2 cups)
  white vinegar

1. Combine the chillies and garlic in a small food processor
   and process until finely chopped.

2. Combine the sugar and vinegar in a saucepan and place
   over low heat, stirring until the sugar dissolves. Add the
   chilli mixture and increase the heat to medium. Cook for
   20 minutes, or until thickened.

3. Pour the hot sauce into warm sterilised bottles or jars
   and seal immediately. Store in a cool, dark place for up
   to 12 months. Refrigerate after opening.

COOK'S NOTE

*If you prefer a milder sauce, remove the seeds from some or
all of the chillies. For an authentic Asian flavour you can
add 1 tablespoon of fish sauce to the vinegar mixture.*

CHILLI DIPPING SAUCE

Makes 750 ml (25 fl oz/3 cups)

8 garlic cloves, roughly
  chopped
12 red bird's eye chillies,
  seeded and roughly
  chopped
345 g (12 oz/1½ cups)
  caster (superfine) sugar
250 ml (8½ fl oz/1 cup)
  fish sauce
250 ml (8½ fl oz/1 cup)
  rice vinegar
125 ml (4 fl oz/½ cup)
  lime juice

1. Combine the garlic and chilli in a small food processor
   and process until finely chopped.

2. Combine the remaining ingredients in a saucepan and
   place over low heat, stirring until the sugar dissolves. Add
   the garlic and chilli mixture and simmer for 5 minutes.

3. Pour the hot sauce into warm sterilised jars and seal
   immediately. Store in a cool, dark place for up to
   12 months. Refrigerate after opening.

COOK'S NOTE

*This delicious sauce is ideal with spring rolls and rice-paper
rolls or as a dressing for salads.*

HORSERADISH CREAM

Makes 125 ml (4 fl oz/½ cup) grated horseradish

1. Trim and peel the horseradish and finely grate it. Put it into a small jar.

2. Heat the vinegar, lemon juice and sugar in a small saucepan over low heat, stirring until the sugar dissolves. Remove from the heat and pour over the horseradish.

3. Store in the refrigerator for up to 1 month. To serve, mix with sour cream to taste.

COOK'S NOTE

Serve horseradish cream with roast beef or roast potatoes, stir it through mashed potato, or serve it with grilled fish. Take care when grating the fresh root as the fumes can be potent – it is best to do it in a well-ventilated area so your eyes don't stream with water. You can use a small food processor to make the job easy – although you may need to add a little water to the horseradish to loosen it.

10 cm (4 in) piece of
  horseradish
80 ml (2½ fl oz/⅓ cup)
  white-wine vinegar
1 tablespoon lemon juice
1 tablespoon caster
  (superfine) sugar
sour cream to serve

PINEAPPLE AND JALAPEÑO SALSA

Makes 600 g (1 lb 5 oz/3 cups)

1 kg (2 lb 3 oz) pineapple, peeled, cored and finely chopped

5 g (¼ oz/¼ cup) mint leaves, torn

1–2 jalapeño chillies, finely sliced

2 spring onions (scallions), finely chopped

juice of 1 lime

1. Mix the ingredients together in a bowl. Serve with fish, prawns or chicken. This salsa can be stored in an airtight container in the refrigerator for up to 1 week.

MANGO AND COCONUT SALSA

Makes 2 cups

1 tablespoon shredded
   coconut
2 mangoes, flesh chopped
1 long red chilli, seeded if
   desired, finely chopped
50 g (2 oz/1 cup) baby basil
   leaves
2 tablespoons snipped chives
1 lime, zested and juiced

1. Toast the coconut in a dry frying pan over low heat for
   1–2 minutes, stirring, until lightly golden. Set aside to cool.

2. Mix the coconut with the remaining ingredients in a bowl.
   If you're not serving the salsa straight away, you can leave
   the coconut out and cover and refrigerate the salsa for
   1–2 days, stirring in the coconut just before serving.
   Serve with curries or as a topping for salmon or chicken.

PAPAYA, LIME AND CHILLI SALSA

Makes 3 cups

1. Mix the ingredients together in a bowl. Serve with fish, fish cakes or chicken. This salsa can be stored in the refrigerator for 1–2 days.

550 g (1 lb 4 oz/3 cups) diced papaya
1 long green chilli, seeded if desired, finely sliced
½ small red onion, finely chopped
25 g (1 oz/½ cup) chopped coriander (cilantro)
juice of 1 lime
1 tablespoon extra-virgin olive oil

CHARGRILLED CORN AND BEAN SALSA

Makes 4 cups

4 corn cobs in husks
1 red capsicum (bell pepper)
400 g (14 oz) tinned black
  beans, rinsed and drained
1 small red onion, finely
  chopped
15 g (½ oz/½ cup)
  chopped parsley
juice of 1 lime
60 ml (2 fl oz/¼ cup)
  extra-virgin olive oil
salt and pepper
25 g (1 oz/¼ cup)
  grated parmesan

1. Preheat a barbecue or chargrill pan to high and cook the corn cobs for 10–15 minutes, turning regularly, until the husks are charred. At the same time cook the capsicum, turning, until blistered. Remove the capsicum and corn from the heat. Put the capsicum in a bowl, cover with plastic wrap and leave to cool (the steam helps loosen the skin).

2. Remove the husks from the corn and use a sharp knife to cut the kernels from the cobs. Put the kernels into a large bowl. Peel the capsicum and remove the seeds. Chop the flesh and add to the corn.

3. Add the beans, onion, parsley, lime juice and oil to the bowl and season well with salt and pepper. Toss to combine. Stir in the parmesan just before serving (the salsa can be eaten immediately, or stored in the refrigerator for up to 3–4 days).

COOK'S NOTE

You can serve this wonderful salsa with almost anything – try it with tacos, enchiladas, quesadillas or nachos, or alongside steak, chicken or fish.

CHUTNEYS AND RELISHES

SPICY EGGPLANT
CHUTNEY
240

APPLE AND SAGE
CHUTNEY
243

GREEN TOMATO
CHUTNEY
244

MANGO CHUTNEY
244

INDIAN TOMATO
CHUTNEY
246

NECTARINE AND
LEMON MYRTLE CHUTNEY
248

MUSTARD PICKLES
250

MOROCCAN LIME
PICKLE
251

ZUCCHINI AND
LIME PICKLES
253

BEETROOT RELISH
254

CELERY AND
WALNUT RELISH
255

ROASTED TOMATO,
CORN AND
TARRAGON RELISH
258

PINEAPPLE AND
GINGER RELISH
259

SPICY EGGPLANT CHUTNEY

Makes 1.25 litres (42 fl oz/5 cups)

1 onion, roughly chopped

4 long red chillies, seeded if
desired, roughly chopped

4 garlic cloves, roughly
chopped

1 tablespoon ground cumin

1 tablespoon ground
coriander

2 teaspoons wholegrain
mustard

60 ml (2 fl oz/¼ cup)
olive oil

1 kg (2 lb 3 oz) eggplants
(aubergines), diced

2 red capsicums (bell
peppers), seeded and
chopped

185 g (6½ oz/1 cup)
soft brown sugar

190 ml (6½ fl oz/¾ cup)
brown (malt) vinegar

1. Combine the onion, chilli and garlic in a small food
   processor and process until finely chopped. Add the
   spices and mustard and pulse to combine.

2. Heat the oil in a large saucepan over medium heat.
   Add the onion mixture and fry for 5 minutes, or until
   fragrant, stirring often. Stir in the eggplant, capsicum,
   sugar and vinegar and bring to the boil. Simmer for
   30 minutes, or until thick, stirring regularly.

3. Ladle the hot chutney into warm sterilised jars and
   seal immediately. Store in a cool, dark place for up
   to 12 months. Refrigerate after opening.

COOK'S NOTE

*Spicy eggplant chutney and Mango chutney (see page 244)
are favourite accompaniments to curries of all sorts. They also
team well with cold meats and are delicious in sandwiches.*

Mango Chutney

Spicy Eggplant Chutney

APPLE AND SAGE CHUTNEY

Makes 1 litre (34 fl oz/4 cups)

1. Combine all the ingredients in a large saucepan and bring to the boil over medium heat, stirring until the sugar dissolves. Cook for 20–25 minutes, until the apple is tender and the mixture has thickened slightly.

2. Ladle the hot chutney into warm sterilised jars and seal immediately. Store in a cool, dark place for up to 12 months. Refrigerate after opening.

2 kg (4 lb 6 oz) tart cooking apples, peeled, cored and cut into wedges
1 onion, finely chopped
2 garlic cloves, finely chopped
2 cinnamon sticks
¼ teaspoon cayenne pepper
6 sage leaves
460 g (1 lb/2 cups) caster (superfine) sugar
500 ml (17 fl oz/2 cups) apple-cider vinegar

GREEN TOMATO CHUTNEY

Makes 1.5 litres (50 fl oz/6 cups)

2 kg (4 lb 6 oz) firm green
    tomatoes, chopped
125 g (4 oz/1 cup) sultanas
    (golden raisins)
2 tart cooking apples, peeled,
    cored and chopped
4 cm (1½ in) piece of ginger,
    grated
1 lemon, chopped and seeded
½ teaspoon cayenne pepper
370 g (13 oz/2 cups) soft
    brown sugar
500 ml (17 fl oz/2 cups)
    brown (malt) vinegar

1. Combine all the ingredients in a large saucepan and
   bring to the boil. Reduce to a simmer and cook, stirring
   occasionally, for 2 hours, or until the chutney has thickened.

2. Ladle the hot chutney into warm sterilised jars and
   seal immediately. Store in a cool, dark place for up to
   12 months. Refrigerate after opening.

MANGO CHUTNEY

Makes 1.25 litres (42 fl oz/5 cups)

460 g (1 lb/2 cups) caster
    (superfine) sugar
500 ml (17 fl oz/2 cups)
    brown (malt) vinegar
2 garlic cloves, crushed
1 teaspoon ground ginger
1 teaspoon yellow mustard
    seeds
6 mangoes, flesh sliced
60 g (2 oz/½ cup) sultanas
    (golden raisins)

1. Combine the sugar, vinegar, garlic and spices in a
   large saucepan and place over low heat. Stir until the
   sugar dissolves, then increase the heat and cook for
   15–20 minutes, until reduced and slightly thickened.

2. Add the mango and sultanas and simmer for another
   10 minutes.

3. Ladle the hot chutney into warm sterilised jars and
   seal immediately. Store in a cool, dark place for up to
   12 months. Refrigerate after opening.

INDIAN TOMATO CHUTNEY

Makes 1 litre (34 fl oz/4 cups)

60 ml (2 fl oz/¼ cup)
  olive oil
1 teaspoon brown mustard
  seeds
2 onions, chopped
4 garlic cloves, finely
  chopped
2 kg (4 lb 6 oz) tomatoes,
  thickly sliced
2 cm (¾ in) piece of fresh
  turmeric, grated (or
  2 teaspoons ground
  turmeric)
6 curry leaves
345 g (12 oz/1½ cups) caster
  (superfine) sugar
375 ml (12½ fl oz/1½ cups)
  white vinegar

1. Heat the oil in a large saucepan over medium heat. Fry the
    mustard seeds for 1 minute, until beginning to pop, then
    add the onion and garlic and fry for 5 minutes, stirring,
    until the onion is soft.

2. Add the remaining ingredients and bring to the boil,
    stirring until the sugar dissolves. Simmer for 30–40 minutes,
    until thickened.

3. Ladle the hot chutney into warm sterilised jars and
    seal immediately. Store in a cool, dark place for up to
    12 months. Refrigerate after opening.

NECTARINE AND LEMON MYRTLE CHUTNEY

Makes 500 ml (17 fl oz/2 cups)

1 kg (2 lb 3 oz) nectarines, peeled if desired, stoned and cut into wedges

1 onion, finely chopped

1 orange, zested and juiced

4 fresh lemon myrtle leaves (or dried leaves, lightly crushed)

185 g (6½ oz/1 cup) soft brown sugar

250 ml (8½ fl oz/1 cup) apple-cider vinegar

1. Combine all the ingredients in a large saucepan and bring to the boil. Cook over medium heat for 30 minutes, stirring occasionally, or until the nectarines are tender and the mixture is thick.

2. Ladle the hot chutney into warm sterilised jars and seal immediately. Store in a cool, dark place for up to 12 months. Refrigerate after opening.

COOK'S NOTE

Lemon myrtle has a delightfully spicy citrus flavour and perfume. You can use fresh or dried leaves in this recipe – if using dried, they can be crushed using a mortar and pestle. Use peaches instead of nectarines if preferred.

MUSTARD PICKLES

Makes 1 litre (34 fl oz/4 cups)

1 small cauliflower, cut
   into small florets
3 small cucumbers, quartered
   lengthways, seeded and
   chopped
6 celery stalks, chopped
2 red capsicums (bell
   peppers), seeded and
   chopped
1 onion, finely chopped
60 g (2 oz/¼ cup) salt
230 g (8 oz/1 cup) caster
   (superfine) sugar
250 ml (8½ fl oz/1 cup)
   white vinegar
2 tablespoons cumin seeds,
   toasted
2 tablespoons cornflour
   (cornstarch)
1 tablespoon mustard powder
1 teaspoon ground turmeric

1. Combine the vegetables including the onion in a large
   heatproof, non-reactive bowl and scatter with the salt. Cover
   with boiling water and leave to soak for 2 hours. The salting
   will prevent the vegetables from collapsing in the pickles.

2. Drain and rinse the vegetables well under cold water.
   Combine the sugar, vinegar and cumin seeds in a large
   saucepan and bring to the boil, stirring until the sugar
   dissolves. Add the drained vegetables and simmer for
   10 minutes, until just tender.

3. Mix the cornflour with the mustard powder, turmeric and
   60 ml (2 fl oz/¼ cup) of water to form a paste. Add to the
   vegetables and simmer for 5 minutes, until thickened.

4. Ladle the hot pickles into warm sterilised jars and
   seal immediately. Store in a cool, dark place for up to
   12 months. Refrigerate after opening.

COOK'S NOTE

*These traditional yellow pickles are thickened with
cornflour (cornstarch), and are great on sandwiches or
served with ham or corned beef.*

MOROCCAN LIME PICKLE

Makes 500 ml (17 fl oz/2 cups)

1. Combine all the ingredients in a large saucepan. Heat gently, stirring, until the sugar dissolves, then increase the heat and bring to the boil. Cook for 30 minutes, or until the limes have collapsed and the mixture has thickened.

2. Ladle the hot pickle into warm sterilised jars and seal immediately. Store in a cool, dark place for up to 12 months. Refrigerate after opening.

COOK'S NOTE

Serve Moroccan lime pickle with cajun chicken or fish, or stir it through a tagine or curry at the end of cooking.

500 g (1 lb 2 oz) limes, quartered and finely sliced
230 g (8 oz/1 cup) caster (superfine) sugar
60 g (2 oz/¼ cup) wholegrain mustard
1 tablespoon Moroccan seasoning
2 teaspoons salt
1 teaspoon fennel seeds
125 ml (4 fl oz/½ cup) water

ZUCCHINI AND LIME PICKLES

Makes 1 litre (34 fl oz/4 cups)

1. Combine the zucchini and onion in a large colander. Sprinkle on the salt and toss well. Place the colander over a large bowl and refrigerate overnight. Discard the juices that drip into the bowl.

2. Combine the sugar, vinegar, lime juice, mustard powder and mustard seeds in a large saucepan and place over low heat, stirring until the sugar dissolves. Increase the heat to high and boil for 10 minutes. Add the zucchini and onion and boil for another 5 minutes. Add the cornflour paste and cook briefly, until the mixture thickens slightly.

3. Ladle the hot pickles into warm sterilised jars and seal immediately. Store in a cool, dark place for up to 12 months. Refrigerate after opening.

1 kg (2 lb 3 oz) zucchini (courgettes), finely sliced (use a mixture of yellow and green zucchini if desired)

1 onion, finely sliced

1 tablespoon salt

345 g (12 oz/1½ cups) caster (superfine) sugar

250 ml (8½ fl oz/1 cup) white vinegar

250 ml (8½ fl oz/1 cup) lime juice

2 teaspoons mustard powder

1 teaspoon yellow mustard seeds

2 tablespoons cornflour (cornstarch) mixed to a paste with 2 tablespoons water

BEETROOT RELISH

Makes 500 ml (17 fl oz/2 cups)

2 tablespoons vegetable oil
2 onions, chopped
1 teaspoon ground allspice
½ teaspoon chilli flakes
8 beetroot (beets), peeled
  and grated
345 g (12 oz/1½ cups) caster
  (superfine) sugar
500 ml (17 fl oz/2 cups)
  apple-cider vinegar

1. Heat the oil in a large saucepan over medium heat. Add the onion and fry for 5 minutes until soft, then add the allspice and chilli flakes and continue to fry for another minute until fragrant. Stir in the beetroot, sugar and vinegar and bring to the boil, stirring until the sugar dissolves. Simmer for 15–20 minutes, until the mixture has thickened slightly.

2. Ladle the hot relish into warm sterilised jars and seal immediately. Store in a cool, dark place for up to 12 months. Refrigerate after opening.

CELERY AND WALNUT RELISH

Makes 2 litres (68 fl oz/8 cups)

1. Heat the oil in a large saucepan over medium heat. Fry the onion for 10–15 minutes with the lid on, stirring often, until soft and caramelised. Stir in the mustard followed by the remaining ingredients. Bring to the boil, stirring until the sugar dissolves, then simmer for 1 hour.

2. Ladle the hot relish into warm sterilised jars and seal immediately. Store in a cool, dark place for up to 12 months. Refrigerate after opening. This relish is excellent served with cold meats.

2 tablespoons olive or walnut oil
2 onions, sliced
2 teaspoons dijon mustard
1 bunch celery, chopped (including leaves)
3 carrots, diced
4 tomatoes, chopped
60 g (2 oz/½ cup) walnuts
230 g (8 oz/1 cup) caster (superfine) sugar
500 ml (17 fl oz/2 cups) apple-cider vinegar

Beetroot
Relish

Roasted Tomato,
Corn and
Tarragon Relish

Pineapple and
Ginger Relish

Celery and
Walnut Relish

ROASTED TOMATO, CORN AND TARRAGON RELISH

Makes 500 ml (17 fl oz/2 cups)

1 kg (2 lb 3 oz) tomatoes,
quartered
1 garlic bulb
3 tarragon sprigs, leaves
stripped from the stems
2 tablespoons raspberry
vinegar
60 ml (2 fl oz/¼ cup)
extra-virgin olive oil
salt and pepper
1 tablespoon yellow mustard
seeds
4 corn cobs, kernels removed
95 g (3½ oz/½ cup) soft
brown sugar
125 ml (4 fl oz/½ cup)
red-wine vinegar

1. Preheat the oven to 200°C/180°C fan-forced (400°F/350°F).
   Put the tomatoes on a large tray lined with baking paper.
   Nestle the garlic bulb into the tomatoes. Scatter over the
   tarragon leaves, drizzle with the vinegar and two-thirds
   of the oil, and season well with salt and pepper. Roast for
   45 minutes, or until the tomatoes are soft and browned.
   Set aside to cool.

2. Peel the skins from the tomato pieces – these should be
   very loose and almost falling off. Squeeze the garlic cloves
   from their skins.

3. Heat the remaining oil in a large saucepan over medium
   heat. Fry the mustard seeds for 1 minute, until beginning
   to pop, then tip in the tomato pieces, garlic and juices from
   the paper. Add the corn kernels, sugar and vinegar. Bring
   to the boil, then simmer for 15 minutes, or until thickened.

4. Ladle the hot relish into warm sterilised jars and seal
   immediately. Store in a cool, dark place for up to
   12 months. Refrigerate after opening.

COOK'S NOTE

*Roasting the tomatoes and garlic gives this relish a
caramelised flavour. It is great served with steak or
sausages.*

PINEAPPLE AND GINGER RELISH

Makes 250 ml (8½ fl oz/1 cup)

1. Heat the oil in a large saucepan over medium heat. Add the onion and fry for 5 minutes, until softened, then add the ginger and chilli and fry for another 30 seconds, until fragrant. Stir in the remaining ingredients and bring to the boil, then reduce the heat and simmer for 30 minutes, or until the pineapple is soft and the mixture has thickened.

2. Ladle the hot relish into warm sterilised jars and seal immediately. Store in a cool, dark place for up to 12 months. Refrigerate after opening.

1 tablespoon olive oil
1 onion, finely chopped
2 tablespoons grated ginger
1 long red chilli, seeded if
  desired, finely sliced
1 medium pineapple
  (weighing about 850 g/
  1 lb 14 oz), peeled, cored
  and chopped
1 red capsicum (bell pepper),
  seeded and finely chopped
370 g (13 oz/2 cups) soft
  brown sugar
500 ml (17 fl oz/2 cups)
  brown (malt) vinegar

CARAMELISED ONION AND THYME JAM

Makes 500 ml (17 fl oz/2 cups)

60 ml (2 fl oz/¼ cup)
  olive oil
1 kg (2 lb 3 oz) red or brown
  onions, finely sliced
1 tablespoon thyme leaves
2 teaspoons dijon mustard
185 g (6½ oz/1 cup) soft
  brown sugar
125 ml (4 fl oz/½ cup)
  balsamic vinegar

1. Heat the oil in a large saucepan over medium heat.
    Add the onion and thyme and fry with the lid on, stirring
    regularly, for 20–30 minutes, until very soft and golden.
    Stir in the mustard followed by the sugar and vinegar and
    reduce the heat to low. Simmer for 15 minutes, or until
    thick and jam-like.

2. Spoon the hot jam into warm sterilised jars and seal
    immediately. Store in a cool, dark place for up to
    12 months. Refrigerate after opening.

PLUM HAM JAM

Makes 500 ml (17 fl oz/2 cups)

1 tablespoon olive oil

1 onion, finely chopped

1 garlic clove, finely chopped

2 teaspoons dijon mustard

1 kg (2 lb 3 oz) plums of
any variety, stoned and
quartered

2 cinnamon sticks

2 star anise

1 red bird's eye chilli

185 g (6½ oz/1 cup)
soft brown sugar

60 ml (2 fl oz/¼ cup)
orange juice

250 ml (8½ fl oz/1 cup)
raspberry or red-wine
vinegar

1. Heat the oil in a large saucepan over medium heat. Fry the onion for 5 minutes until softened, then add the garlic and fry for another 30 seconds until fragrant. Stir in the mustard, followed by the plums, spices (including the whole chilli) and remaining ingredients. Bring to the boil, then simmer for 25–30 minutes, until thickened.

2. Ladle the hot jam into warm sterilised jars and seal immediately. Store in a cool, dark place for up to 12 months. Refrigerate after opening.

COOK'S NOTE

I use this delicious jam not only to glaze baked ham, but also to baste roast turkey or chicken and even fish! You can replace the plums with cherries, peaches or nectarines if you like.

CHILLI JAM

Makes 500 ml (17 fl oz/2 cups)

1. Combine the chilli, onion, garlic and ginger in a food processor and process to a paste.

2. Heat the oil in a large saucepan over medium heat and add the paste. Fry for 10 minutes, stirring frequently, or until golden. Add the sugar, vinegar and fish sauce and bring to the boil. Simmer gently for 30–40 minutes, stirring occasionally, until thick and glossy – a line drawn in the jam should hold its shape for a few seconds. If it doesn't, simmer for another 5 minutes before trying again.

3. Spoon the hot jam into warm sterilised jars and seal immediately. Store in a cool, dark place for up to 12 months. Refrigerate after opening.

COOK'S NOTE

The desired heat of chilli jam is a personal choice; my family prefers it mild so I use long red chillies and remove the seeds. If you prefer more fire, use hotter chillies, or a mixture of hot and mild, and leave some or all of the seeds in. One more thing – use gloves when preparing chillies, and make sure the kitchen is well ventilated when cooking the jam – there will be tears! Use chilli jam as a base for stir-fries and curries and as a marinade for fish, chicken or prawns (shrimp), or try spreading a thin layer on toast and topping with bacon and eggs!

500 g (1 lb 2 oz) long red chillies, seeded and roughly chopped
3 onions, roughly chopped
6 garlic cloves, roughly chopped
1 tablespoon grated ginger
2 tablespoons peanut or vegetable oil
280 g (10 oz/1½ cups) soft brown sugar
250 ml (8½ fl oz/1 cup) brown (malt) vinegar
125 ml (4 fl oz/½ cup) fish sauce

MIXED BERRY JAM

Makes 1 litre (34 fl oz/4 cups)

1 kg (2 lb 3 oz) mixed berries such as strawberries, raspberries, blackberries and mulberries, hulled as necessary
690 g (1½ lb/3 cups) caster (superfine) sugar
2 lemons, juiced (skin, pith and seeds reserved)

1. Put a layer of berries into a bowl or dish and sprinkle with some of the sugar. Top with another layer of berries and sugar. Repeat until all the berries and sugar have been used, then cover and refrigerate overnight. The sugar will extract juice from the berries.

2. Transfer the mixture to a large saucepan and add the lemon juice. Place the lemon skins, pith and seeds on a piece of muslin (cheesecloth). Bring in the corners of the muslin and tie with a long piece of kitchen string to make a bag. Tie to the handle of the saucepan, allowing it to drop into the berries.

3. Bring the mixture to the boil and cook for 30–40 minutes, skimming foam from the surface as necessary, until the jam is at setting point. This can be tested by putting a teaspoon of the jam onto a chilled plate; the jam should appear firm with a wrinkle on the surface once it cools.

4. Discard the muslin bag, ladle the hot jam into warm sterilised jars and seal immediately. Store in a cool, dark place for up to 12 months. Refrigerate after opening.

COOK'S NOTE

*For a quick **microwave berry jam,** combine 300 g (10½ oz) of mixed berries and 2 tablespoons of lemon juice in a large heatproof bowl and microwave on high for 5 minutes. Stir in 230 g (8 oz/1 cup) of caster (superfine) sugar and microwave for 3 minutes. Give the mixture a stir, then microwave for another 3 minutes. Test for setting by putting a teaspoon of jam onto a chilled plate; the jam should appear firm with a wrinkle on the surface once it cools. If not, cook for another 3 minutes, or until set. Makes 250 ml (8½ fl oz/1 cup).*

Mixed Berry Jam

Apricot Jam

APRICOT JAM

Makes 1.25 litres (42 fl oz/5 cups)

1 kg (2 lb 3 oz) apricots,
    stoned and quartered
    (stones reserved)
2 tablespoons lemon juice
125 ml (4 fl oz/½ cup) water
1 kg (2 lb 3 oz/4⅓ cups)
    caster (superfine) sugar

1. Put the apricot stones in a zip-lock bag and tap lightly with a mallet or rolling pin to crack the shells and expose the kernels inside. Put the kernels on a small piece of muslin (cheesecloth), bring in the corners and tie with a long piece of kitchen string to make a bag.

2. Combine the apricots, lemon juice and water in a large saucepan and place over medium heat. Cover with a lid and bring to the boil. Cook for 5–10 minutes, until the apricots have softened slightly.

3. Add the sugar and stir over low heat until the sugar dissolves. Tie the bag of kernels to the handle of the saucepan, allowing it to drop into the apricots. Increase the heat to high and boil for 20–30 minutes, skimming foam from the surface as necessary, until the jam is at setting point. This can be tested by putting a teaspoon of the jam onto a chilled plate; the jam should appear firm with a wrinkle on the surface once it cools.

4. Discard the muslin bag, ladle the hot jam into warm sterilised jars and seal immediately. Store in a cool, dark place for up to 12 months. Refrigerate after opening.

ROSELLA AND APPLE JAM

Makes 500 ml (17 fl oz/2 cups)

1. Use an apple corer to gently push through the base of each rosella to cut out the green seed pod inside. Pop the pods and red fleshy calyxes into separate bowls. Wash both well.

2. Place the pods in a saucepan with generous water to cover and simmer for 20 minutes. Strain the liquid through a fine-mesh sieve, discarding the pods. This liquid contains pectin.

3. Combine the calyxes, apple, lemon juice and 500 ml (17 fl oz/2 cups) of the seed-pod liquid in a clean saucepan. Bring to the boil, then reduce the heat to medium, cover with a lid and cook for 20–30 minutes, until the rosellas start to soften. Remove from the heat, then carefully pour into a measuring jug to measure the mixture in cups. Return the mixture to the pan and add equal cups of sugar.

4. Place the pan over low heat, stirring until the sugar dissolves. Increase the heat to medium and cook for 30–35 minutes, regularly skimming foam from the surface, until the jam is at setting point. This can be tested by putting a teaspoon of the jam onto a chilled plate; the jam should appear firm with a wrinkle on the surface once it cools.

5. Ladle the hot jam into warm sterilised jars and seal immediately. Store in a cool, dark place for up to 12 months. Refrigerate after opening.

COOK'S NOTE

Rosellas have a tart flavour similar to raspberries or rhubarb. To add something special to this delicious jam, include 250 ml (8½ fl oz/1 cup) of pink sparkling wine in addition to the seed-pod liquid (the jam will end up slightly more syrupy).

500 g (1 lb 2 oz) fresh rosellas
2 tart cooking apples, peeled, cored and chopped
juice of 1 lemon
caster (superfine) sugar

Fig and Vanilla
Conserve

Strawberry and
Basil Conserve

STRAWBERRY AND BASIL CONSERVE

Makes 875 ml (30 fl oz/3½ cups)

1. Put a layer of the strawberries into a bowl or dish and sprinkle with some of the sugar. Top with another layer of strawberries and sugar. Repeat until all the strawberries and sugar have been used, then cover and refrigerate overnight. The sugar will extract juice from the strawberries.

2. Transfer the mixture to a large saucepan and add the lemon juice. Place the lemon skins, pith and seeds and the basil on a piece of muslin (cheesecloth). Bring in the corners of the muslin and tie with a long piece of kitchen string to make a bag. Tie to the handle of the saucepan, allowing it to drop into the strawberry mixture.

3. Boil for 20–30 minutes, skimming foam from the surface as necessary, until the conserve is at setting point. This can be tested by putting a teaspoon of the conserve onto a chilled plate; the conserve should appear firm with a wrinkle on the surface once it cools.

4. Discard the muslin bag, ladle the hot conserve into warm sterilised jars and seal immediately. Store in a cool, dark place for up to 12 months. Refrigerate after opening.

COOK'S NOTE

*I'm often asked the difference between conserves and jams –
a conserve is simply made with whole or sliced fruit, which
makes it chunkier.*

1 kg (2 lb 3 oz) strawberries, hulled

690 g (1½ lb/3 cups) caster (superfine) sugar

2 lemons, juiced (skin, pith and seeds reserved)

15 g (½ oz/¼ cup) basil leaves

CITRUS MARMALADE

Makes 1 litre (34 fl oz/4 cups)

500 g (1 lb 2 oz) oranges
500 g (1 lb 2 oz) mandarins
500 g (1 lb 2 oz) limes
2 litres (68 fl oz/8 cups)
  water
2 kg (4 lb 6 oz) caster
  (superfine) sugar
juice of 2 lemons

1. Combine the whole fruit and water in a pot. Cover with a lid and simmer for 1–2 hours, until the fruit is tender.

2. Use a slotted spoon to remove the fruit from the liquid. Cut the fruit into slices and pick out as many seeds as you can, returning them to the cooking liquid (the seeds contain pectin for setting the jam). Simmer the liquid for another 20 minutes, then strain the liquid and discard the seeds.

3. Measure the sliced fruit in cups and add enough strained liquid to make it up to a total of 1.5 litres (50 fl oz/6 cups). Return the fruit and liquid to the clean pot. Add the sugar and lemon juice and stir over low heat until the sugar dissolves. Increase the heat and boil for 30–35 minutes, skimming foam from the surface as necessary, until the marmalade is at setting point. This can be tested by putting a teaspoon of the marmalade onto a chilled plate; the marmalade should appear firm with a wrinkle on the surface once it cools.

4. Ladle the hot marmalade into warm sterilised jars and seal immediately. Store in a cool, dark place for up to 12 months. Refrigerate after opening.

COOK'S NOTE

This recipe makes a chunky marmalade – if you prefer yours smoother, just chop up the fruit.

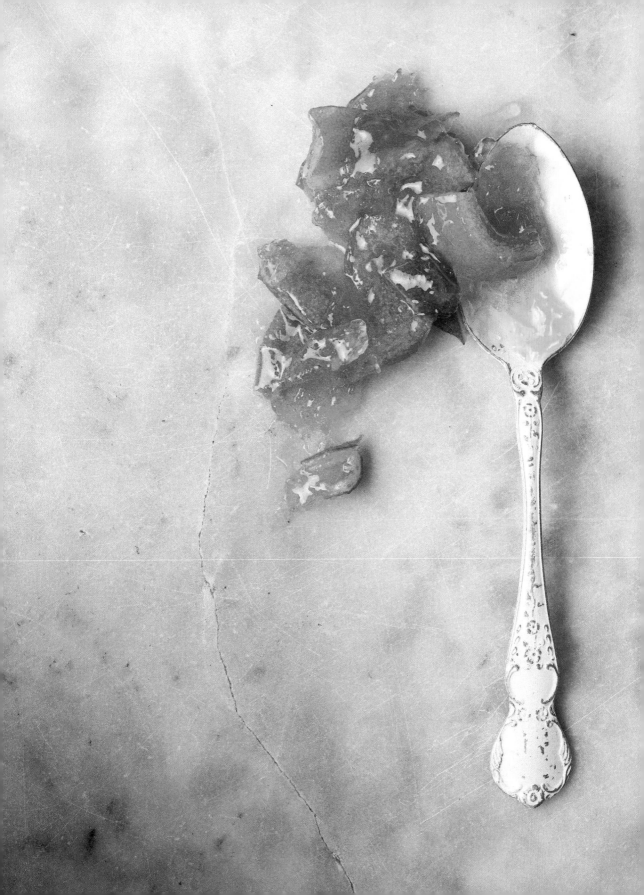

FIG AND VANILLA CONSERVE

Makes 500 ml (17 fl oz/2 cups)

1 kg (2 lb 3 oz) figs, halved
(see Cook's note)
690 g (1½ lb/3 cups) caster
(superfine) sugar
1 lemon, juiced (skin, pith
and seeds reserved)
1 vanilla bean, split
lengthways and seeds
scraped

1. Put a layer of figs into a bowl or dish and sprinkle with some of the sugar. Top with another layer of figs and sugar. Repeat until all the figs and sugar have been used, then cover and refrigerate overnight. The sugar will extract juice from the figs.

2. Transfer the mixture to a large saucepan and add the lemon juice and vanilla seeds.

3. Place the lemon skins, pith and seeds on a piece of muslin (cheesecloth). Bring in the corners of the muslin and tie with a long piece of kitchen string to make a bag. Tie to the handle of the saucepan, allowing the bag to drop into the fig mixture.

4. Bring to the boil and cook for 20–30 minutes, skimming foam from the surface as necessary, until the conserve is at setting point. This can be tested by putting a teaspoon of the conserve onto a chilled plate; the conserve should appear firm with a wrinkle on the surface once it cools.

5. Discard the muslin bag, ladle the hot conserve into warm sterilised jars and seal immediately. Store in a cool, dark place for up to 12 months. Refrigerate after opening.

COOK'S NOTE

Some figs have thick skins, which can be peeled. To do this, hold a fig in one hand and insert a small paring knife under the skin at the top of the fig. Peel the skin away in strips, taking care not to remove too much of the soft, sweet flesh.

CRAB-APPLE AND ROSEMARY JELLY

Makes 375 ml (12½ fl oz/1½ cups)

1. Combine the crab-apples, rosemary sprigs, lemon juice and water in a large saucepan. Bring to the boil then reduce the heat, cover with a lid and simmer for 30 minutes, or until the crab-apples are very soft. Allow to cool slightly.

2. Strain the liquid through a colander into a large bowl, jug or saucepan and discard the solids. Line a strainer with muslin (cheesecloth) and place it on top of a measuring jug. Pour in the liquid, straining it for a second time. It takes a while for the liquid to drip through the muslin, but be patient – trying to hurry it up can make the jelly cloudy. Measure the liquid in cups, then return it to the clean saucepan with equal cups of sugar.

3. Place the pan over low heat, stirring until the sugar dissolves. Increase the heat to high and cook for 30–35 minutes, skimming foam from the surface as necessary, until the jelly is at setting point. This can be tested by putting a teaspoon of the jelly onto a chilled plate; the jelly should appear firm with a wrinkle on the surface once it cools.

4. Ladle the hot jelly into warm sterilised jars and seal immediately. Store in a cool, dark place for up to 12 months. Refrigerate after opening.

600 g (1 lb 5 oz) crab-apples, halved
4 rosemary sprigs
juice of 1 lemon
750 ml (25 fl oz/3 cups) water
caster (superfine) sugar

CRAB-APPLE AND CHILLI PASTE

Makes 375 ml (12½ fl oz/1½ cups)

600 g (1 lb 5 oz) crab-apples, halved
juice of 1 lemon
750 ml (25 fl oz/3 cups) water
caster (superfine) sugar
1 red bird's eye chilli, halved lengthways

1. Combine the crab-apples, lemon juice and water in a large saucepan. Bring to the boil then reduce the heat, cover and simmer for 30 minutes, or until the crab-apples are very soft.

2. Place a fine-mesh sieve over a bowl and pour in the crab-apple mixture, pushing through as much purée as possible. Discard the solids. Measure the purée in cups. Return the purée to the clean saucepan and add equal cups of sugar, along with the chilli.

3. Place the pan over low heat, stirring until the sugar dissolves. Increase the heat and boil for 45–60 minutes, stirring regularly and skimming foam from the surface as necessary, until very thick – a line drawn in the paste should hold its shape for a few seconds.

4. Spray or brush a small tray with oil and pour in the paste, removing the chilli. Leave to set overnight.

5. Cut the paste into squares, or use a cookie cutter to cut rounds. Place in an airtight container with baking paper between each layer. Store in a cool, dark place for up to 6 months.

COOK'S NOTE

Crab-apple paste is a great alternative to quince paste on a cheese platter. I also use it to glaze roast lamb. You can wrap the paste in cellophane, or even set it in small containers for a delightful gift. (You can omit the chilli if preferred.)

CANDIED CUMQUATS

Makes 500 ml (17 fl oz/2 cups)

460 g (1 lb/2 cups) caster
 (superfine) sugar
500 ml (17 fl oz/2 cups) water
500 g (1 lb 2 oz) cumquats,
 halved or thickly sliced,
 seeds removed if desired
2 cloves

1. Combine the sugar and water in a saucepan and place over low heat, stirring until the sugar dissolves. Bring to the boil, then add the cumquats and cloves and boil for 10 minutes.

2. Reduce the heat to very low and simmer for 20–25 minutes, until the cumquats are translucent and the syrup is thick.

3. Ladle the hot cumquats and syrup into warm sterilised jars and seal immediately. Store in a cool, dark place for up to 12 months. Refrigerate after opening.

COOK'S NOTE

Candied cumquats are delicious served with cheese – especially blue cheese or baked ricotta – or with panna cotta, yoghurt or porridge.

RHUBARB AND LEMON COMPOTE

Makes 750 ml (25 fl oz/3 cups)

500 g (1 lb 2 oz) rhubarb,
cut into 5 cm (2 in) lengths
1 lemon, zest peeled off in
wide strips, juiced
140 g (5 oz/¾ cup) soft
brown sugar
2 cinnamon sticks

1. Combine all the ingredients in a saucepan and bring to the boil, stirring. Reduce the heat and simmer for 10 minutes, or until the rhubarb is soft.

2. Allow to cool, then store in an airtight container in the refrigerator for up to 2 weeks. Alternatively, ladle the hot compote into warm sterilised jars, seal immediately, and heat-process (see page 12), which will extend the shelf life to 12 months.

COOK'S NOTE

A compote is traditionally made from whole or large pieces of fruit cooked with less sugar than a jam or conserve. It is generally used as a topping for ice-cream, pancakes, muesli or yoghurt. You can try different fruit and flavour combinations (ginger, spices, basil, citrus zest and nuts all make interesting additions).

BLUEBERRY TOPPING

Makes 750 ml (25 fl oz/3 cups)

500 g (1 lb 2 oz) blueberries
345 g (12 oz/1½ cups) caster
  (superfine) sugar
1 teaspoon vanilla extract
60 ml (2 fl oz/¼ cup) water

1. Combine all the ingredients in a saucepan and place over low heat, stirring until the sugar dissolves. Increase the heat to medium and cook for 30 minutes, or until syrupy.

2. Remove from the heat and lightly squash the blueberries with the back of a fork. Ladle the hot sauce into warm sterilised jars and seal immediately. Store in a cool, dark place for up to 12 months. Refrigerate after opening.

COOK'S NOTE

Serve this blueberry topping on ice-cream, in trifles, with muesli or stirred through yoghurt.

ROASTED APRICOT AND CINNAMON CURD

Makes 625 ml (21 fl oz/2½ cups)

500 g (1 lb 2 oz) apricots,
  halved and stoned
230 g (8 oz/1 cup) caster
  (superfine) sugar
1 teaspoon ground cinnamon
60 ml (2 fl oz/¼ cup) water
3 eggs plus 1 egg yolk, lightly
  beaten
150 g (5 oz) chilled unsalted
  butter, diced

1. Preheat the oven to 180°C/160°C fan-forced (350°F/320°F) and line a tray with baking paper. Spread the apricots across the tray skin-side down and bake for 30–40 minutes, until soft and golden. Set aside to cool.

2. If desired you can peel the apricots – the skins should be quite loose after roasting. Place the apricots in a blender and blend until smooth, then transfer the purée to a saucepan. Add the sugar, cinnamon and water and place over low heat, stirring until the sugar dissolves. Once dissolved, remove from the heat.

3. Whisk in the beaten eggs and butter until the butter is melted and the mixture is well combined. Return to low heat and cook for about 10 minutes, whisking constantly, until the mixture forms a thick curd. Make sure you remove the curd from the heat before it separates. If you are worried about it separating, you can occasionally remove the pan from the heat while continuing to whisk.

4. Ladle the curd into warm sterilised jars and seal immediately. Store in the refrigerator for up to 3 weeks.

COOK'S NOTE

Fruit curds are smooth, intensely flavoured spreads that can be served on toast, scones or pikelets. They can also fill tarts or be swirled though cake or muffin batters or ice-cream.

PINEAPPLE AND COCONUT CURD

Makes 500 ml (17 fl oz/2 cups)

approximately 250 g (9 oz)
  peeled pineapple
125 ml (4 fl oz/½ cup)
  coconut cream
200 g (7 oz) chilled
  unsalted butter, diced
1 egg plus 7 egg yolks,
  lightly beaten

1. Push the pineapple through a juicer or blend it to a purée in a blender, then strain and measure 125 ml (4 fl oz/½ cup) of juice. Pour into a saucepan and add the coconut cream. Heat until the mixture is hot to touch, then remove from the heat.

2. Whisk in the butter until it melts, then add the beaten egg and whisk until well combined. Return to low heat and cook for 10–15 minutes, whisking constantly, until the mixture forms a thick curd. Make sure you remove the curd from the heat before it separates. If you are worried about it separating, you can occasionally remove the pan from the heat while continuing to whisk.

3. Ladle the curd into warm sterilised jars and seal immediately. Store in the refrigerator for up to 3 weeks.

COOK'S NOTE

To make an easy **microwave passionfruit curd,** *whisk together 4 eggs and 170 g (6 oz/¾ cup) of caster (superfine) sugar in a large heatproof bowl until well combined. Add 125 ml (4 fl oz/½ cup) of passionfruit pulp and 100 g (3½ oz) of diced, chilled unsalted butter. Microwave on medium (50%) for 6–10 minutes, whisking every minute, until thick enough to coat the back of a spoon. Spoon the hot curd into warm sterilised jars, then seal and store in the refrigerator for up to 3 weeks. Makes 440 ml (15 fl oz/1¾ cups).*

PICKLING

PICKLED ONIONS
290

PICKLED GINGER
292

PICKLED
BEETROOT
293

PICKLED
CABBAGE
294

PICKLED
ZUCCHINI
295

PICKLED
CARROT
298

PICKLED
CUCUMBERS
299

PICKLED MIXED
VEGETABLES
300

PICKLED
WATERMELON RIND
301

GHERKINS
304

PICKLED BEANS
WITH LEEKS
305

PICKLED VANILLA
PEACHES
306

PICKLED PEARS
308

SPICED PICKLED
ORANGES WITH LIME
310

PICKLED ONIONS

Makes 2 litres (68 fl oz/8 cups)

1 kg (2 lb 3 oz) small pickling
   onions, peeled and lightly
   trimmed (see Cook's note)
60 g (2 oz/¼ cup) salt
115 g (4 oz/½ cup) caster
   (superfine) sugar
500 ml (17 fl oz/2 cups)
   white-wine vinegar
2 teaspoons coriander seeds
1 teaspoon fennel seeds
4 cardamom pods
2 teaspoons black or white
   peppercorns
4 bay leaves

1. Put the onions in a large non-reactive bowl and scatter with 2 tablespoons of the salt. Cover with water and weight the onions down with a plate, keeping them submerged. Leave to stand at room temperature overnight.

2. Drain the onions and rinse well under cold water, then drain again.

3. Combine the remaining 1 tablespoon of salt, sugar, vinegar, spices, bay leaves and 250 ml (8½ fl oz/1 cup) of water in a large saucepan. Bring to the boil, then reduce the heat and simmer for 5 minutes. Add the onions and simmer for a further 10 minutes.

4. Use a slotted spoon to transfer the hot onions into warm sterilised jars. Cover with the pickling liquid and seal the jars immediately. Store in a cool, dark place for up to 12 months. Refrigerate after opening.

COOK'S NOTE

Eat pickled onions as a snack, or use in place of raw onion when making casseroles, stews or soups. A good trick for peeling the onions easily is to put them in a large heatproof bowl, cover with boiling water and set aside for 15 minutes. This helps soften their skins so they slide off with less effort and tears! Make sure you trim only a little off the onions, as you want them to hold together in one piece.

PICKLED GINGER

Makes 375 ml (12½ fl oz/1½ cups)

250 g (9 oz) young ginger,
  peeled and finely sliced
½ teaspoon salt
55 g (2 oz/¼ cup) caster
  (superfine) sugar
125 ml (4 fl oz/½ cup) rice
  vinegar or white vinegar

1. Combine the ginger and salt in a large bowl and toss well. Transfer to a warm sterilised jar.

2. Combine the sugar and vinegar in a small saucepan and place over low heat, stirring until the sugar dissolves. Bring to the boil, then pour over the ginger and leave to cool. Cover with the lid and refrigerate for at least 24 hours before eating. Store in the refrigerator for up to 2 months.

COOK'S NOTE

Young ginger has thin, pale yellow skin (mature ginger has thicker, drier skin). When pickled, young ginger takes on a pretty pink hue and is great served with sushi, salmon or prawns (shrimp). Use a mandoline to give you the finest slices.

PICKLED BEETROOT

Makes 2 litres (68 fl oz/8 cups)

1. Boil the whole beetroot until tender (the cooking time depends on their size, with medium beetroot taking 30–40 minutes). Drain, and when cool enough to handle, peel and trim the beetroot. Leave whole or thickly slice as desired, and pack into warm sterilised jars.

2. Combine the sugar, vinegar and water in a saucepan. Bring to the boil, stirring until the sugar dissolves. Boil for 5 minutes.

3. Pour the hot liquid over the beetroot, making sure the beetroot is covered. Seal immediately.

4. Stand the jars on a wire rack or trivet in the base of a deep pot. Fill the pot with boiling water to cover the jars by at least 3 cm (1¼ in). Cover with a tight-fitting lid and simmer for 20 minutes. Remove the jars from the water and leave to cool on a wooden board. Store in a cool, dark place for up to 12 months. Refrigerate after opening.

1 kg (2 lb 3 oz) beetroot (beets)
370 g (13 oz/2 cups) soft brown sugar
500 ml (17 fl oz/2 cups) brown (malt) vinegar
250 ml (8½ fl oz/1 cup) water

PICKLED CABBAGE

Makes 2 litres (68 fl oz/8 cups)

1 kg (2 lb 3 oz) cabbage (red or white), finely shredded
80 g (3 oz/⅓ cup) salt
185 g (6½ oz/1 cup) soft brown sugar
1 litre (34 fl oz/4 cups) white vinegar
1 tablespoon yellow mustard seeds
2 teaspoons black peppercorns

1. Put the cabbage into a large non-reactive bowl in layers, salting each layer, until all the cabbage and salt are used. Cover and leave to stand at room temperature for 24 hours.

2. Tip the cabbage into a colander and rinse well under cold water (do so in batches if necessary). Drain the cabbage well then spread out on a few clean tea towels and pat dry.

3. Combine the remaining ingredients in a large saucepan and bring to the boil. Cook rapidly for 5 minutes.

4. Pack the cabbage into warm sterilised jars. Cover with the hot pickling liquid and seal immediately.

5. Stand the jars on a wire rack or trivet in the base of a deep pot. Fill the pot with boiling water to cover the jars by at least 3 cm (1¼ in). Cover with a tight-fitting lid and simmer for 20 minutes. Remove the jars to a wooden board and leave to cool. Store in a cool, dark place for up to 12 months. Refrigerate after opening.

COOK'S NOTE

The two most common ways to pickle cabbage are through natural fermentation, which ends in a product known as sauerkraut (see page 74), and by packing in a hot vinegar solution, as in this recipe. You can use either red or white cabbage, and it can be served as a side dish or as part of a ploughman's lunch.

PICKLED ZUCCHINI

Makes 750 ml (25 fl oz/3 cups)

1. Combine the zucchini and onion in a large non-reactive bowl, then sprinkle on the salt and toss well. Cover and refrigerate overnight.

2. Tip the zucchini and onion into a colander and rinse well under cold water (do so in batches if necessary). Drain well, then pack into warm sterilised jars. Scatter over the peppercorns.

3. Combine the sugar and vinegar in a saucepan and gently bring to the boil, stirring until the sugar dissolves. Simmer for 5 minutes.

4. Pour the hot vinegar mixture over the zucchini and onion, making sure they are covered, then seal the jars immediately. Store in a cool, dark place for up to 12 months. Refrigerate after opening.

750 g (1 lb 10 oz) small–medium zucchini (courgettes) of mixed colours if desired, peeled into long ribbons

1 small red onion, finely sliced

60 g (2 oz/¼ cup) salt

1 teaspoon white peppercorns

230 g (8 oz/1 cup) caster (superfine) sugar

500 ml (17 fl oz/2 cups) white-wine vinegar

Pickled
Beetroot

Pickled
Cabbage

Pickled
Zucchini

Pickled Carrots

Pickled Cucumbers

PICKLED CARROTS

Makes 2 litres (68 fl oz/8 cups)

1 kg (2 lb 3 oz) carrots, trimmed, peeled and quartered lengthways
4 garlic cloves, peeled
2 bay leaves
1 teaspoon black peppercorns
1 teaspoon yellow mustard seeds
115 g (4 oz/½ cup) caster (superfine) sugar
1 litre (34 fl oz/4 cups) white vinegar
1 litre (34 fl oz/4 cups) water

1. Blanch the carrots in a large saucepan of boiling water for 2 minutes, then drain and refresh under cold water.

2. Stand the carrots upright in warm sterilised jars, packing in tightly.

3. Combine the garlic, bay leaves, peppercorns, mustard seeds, sugar, vinegar and water in a large saucepan and bring to the boil, stirring until the sugar dissolves. Pour over the carrots, making sure they are covered. Seal the jars immediately.

4. Stand the jars on a wire rack or trivet in the base of a deep pot. Fill the pot with boiling water to cover the jars by at least 3 cm (1¼ in). Cover with a tight-fitting lid and simmer for 20 minutes. Remove the jars from the water and leave to cool on a wooden board. Store in a cool, dark place for up to 12 months. Refrigerate after opening.

COOK'S NOTE

Enjoy these carrots straight from the jar or as crudités on a platter, or chop them and add to any dish calling for carrot. You can use a mixture of carrot varieties if you have them growing.

PICKLED CUCUMBERS

Makes 1.5 litres (50 fl oz/6 cups)

1. Put the cucumber into a large heatproof, non-reactive bowl. Scatter with the salt, then pour over 1.5 litres (50 fl oz/ 6 cups) of boiling water. Weight down with a plate, keeping the cucumber submerged in the water. Leave to cool, then refrigerate overnight.

2. Drain the cucumber and rinse well under cold water. Drain again.

3. Combine the sugar, vinegar, mustard seeds and peppercorns in a large saucepan and bring to the boil. Boil for 5 minutes, then remove from the heat and stir in the cucumber. Leave to stand for 2 minutes.

4. Use a slotted spoon to transfer the cucumber into warm sterilised jars. Drop 2 whole chillies into each jar and cover with the hot vinegar mixture. Seal immediately.

5. Stand the jars on a wire rack or trivet in the base of a deep pot. Fill the pot with boiling water to cover the jars by at least 3 cm (1¼ in). Cover with a tight-fitting lid and simmer for 20 minutes. Remove the jars to a wooden board and leave to cool. Store in a cool, dark place for up to 12 months. Refrigerate after opening.

COOK'S NOTE

If your cucumbers have grown large and mature in your garden, then this recipe is a great one to make use of them – just peel off their tough skins.

1.5 kg (3 lb 5 oz) cucumbers (see Cook's note), halved lengthways, seeds scooped out and thickly sliced
60 g (2 oz/¼ cup) salt
55 g (2 oz/¼ cup) caster (superfine) sugar
375 ml (12½ fl oz/1½ cups) apple-cider vinegar
1 teaspoon yellow mustard seeds
2 teaspoons black or white peppercorns
red bird's eye chillies

PICKLED MIXED VEGETABLES

Makes 2 litres (68 fl oz/8 cups)

1 small cauliflower, cut into
  small florets
1 small broccoli, cut into
  small florets
125 g (4 oz) small pickling
  onions, peeled and halved
2 carrots, quartered
  lengthways and chopped
200 g (7 oz) green beans,
  cut into 2 cm (¾ in) lengths
1 teaspoon black
  peppercorns
bay leaves
230 g (8 oz/1 cup) caster
  (superfine) sugar
1 litre (34 fl oz/4 cups)
  white vinegar

1. Put the vegetables into warm sterilised jars in layers. Divide the peppercorns between the jars, and insert a bay leaf in each.

2. Combine the sugar and vinegar in a saucepan and gently bring to the boil, stirring until the sugar dissolves. Simmer for 5 minutes, then pour over the vegetables, making sure they are covered. Seal the jars immediately.

3. Stand the jars on a wire rack or trivet in the base of a deep pot. Fill the pot with boiling water to cover the jars by at least 3 cm (1¼ in). Cover with a tight-fitting lid and simmer for 20 minutes. Remove the jars to a wooden board and leave to cool. Store in a cool, dark place for up to 12 months. Refrigerate after opening.

COOK'S NOTE

These pickled vegetables go beautifully on a European-style platter with cold meats and bread. You can even add them (rinsed if desired) to stir-fries and fried rice.

PICKLED WATERMELON RIND

Makes 1.25 litres (42 fl oz/5 cups)

1. Quarter the watermelon and cut the flesh from the rind. Put the flesh aside for another use (see Cook's note). Peel the green skin from the rind and discard. Cut the white rind into squares.

2. Bring a large saucepan of water to the boil, then add the rind and boil for 10 minutes. Drain and transfer to a large non-reactive bowl. Scatter with the salt and cover with cold water. Weight down with a plate, keeping the rind submerged in the water. Leave to stand at room temperature overnight.

3. Combine the sugar, vinegar and 250 ml (8½ fl oz/1 cup) of water in a large saucepan. Gently bring to the boil, stirring until the sugar has dissolved. Add the spices and simmer for 5 minutes, or until syrupy.

4. Drain the watermelon rind and rinse it under cold water. Add to the syrup. Simmer for 1 hour, or until translucent and tender.

5. Ladle the hot pickle into warm sterilised jars and seal immediately. Store in a cool, dark place for up to 12 months. Refrigerate after opening.

3 kg (6 lb 10 oz) watermelon
2 tablespoons salt
460 g (1 lb/2 cups) caster (superfine) sugar
500 ml (17 fl oz/2 cups) apple-cider vinegar
2 cinnamon sticks
4 cloves
2 star anise

COOK'S NOTE

Pickled watermelon rind is well known in America – it's delicious with all sorts of meat and fish. It's also a great way to use up the rind of watermelons from the summer garden. If you're not eating the watermelon flesh immediately, simply juice it or purée it and freeze it. You can make ice cubes for adding to drinks, or try swirling the purée through softened vanilla ice-cream and refreezing.

Picked Mixed Vegetables

Pickled Watermelon Rind

GHERKINS

Makes 2 litres (68 fl oz/8 cups)

1 kg (2 lb 3 oz) small pickling
  cucumbers with stems
  attached
1 litre (34 fl oz/4 cups) water
180 g (6½ oz/¾ cup) salt
1 teaspoon yellow mustard
  seeds
½ teaspoon black or white
  peppercorns
500 ml (17 fl oz/2 cups)
  white vinegar

1. Trim the cucumber stems to about 1 cm (½ in) long.
   Put the cucumbers in a large heatproof, non-reactive bowl.

2. Combine 750 ml (25 fl oz/3 cups) of the water and
   120 g (4 oz/½ cup) of the salt in a saucepan. Bring to
   the boil, then pour over the cucumbers. Weight down
   with a plate, keeping the cucumbers submerged in the
   water. Leave to stand at room temperature overnight.

3. Drain the cucumbers and rinse well under cold water,
   then drain again. Tip onto a clean tea towel and pat the
   cucumbers dry. Pack tightly into warm sterilised jars. Divide
   the mustard seeds and peppercorns between the jars.

4. Heat the vinegar, remaining salt and remaining water in
   a saucepan until boiling, stirring to help the salt dissolve.
   Pour over the cucumbers, making sure they are covered,
   and seal the jars immediately.

5. Stand the jars on a wire rack or trivet in the base of a deep
   pot. Fill the pot with boiling water to cover the jars by at
   least 3 cm (1¼ in). Cover with a tight-fitting lid and simmer
   for 20 minutes. Remove the jars to a wooden board and
   leave to cool. Store in a cool, dark place for up to 12 months.
   Refrigerate after opening.

PICKLED BEANS WITH LEEKS

Makes 2 litres (68 fl oz/8 cups)

1. Blanch the green beans in a large saucepan of boiling water for 2 minutes, then drain, rinse under cold water and drain again. Repeat with the yellow beans and then with the leek.

2. Layer the green beans, yellow beans and leek in warm sterilised jars, packing in tightly.

3. Combine the bay leaves, peppercorns, mustard seeds, sugar, vinegar and water in a large saucepan and bring to the boil, stirring until the sugar dissolves. Pour over the vegetables, making sure they are covered. Seal the jars immediately.

4. Stand the jars on a wire rack or trivet in the base of a deep pot. Fill the pot with boiling water to cover the jars by at least 3 cm (1¼ in). Cover with a tight-fitting lid and simmer for 20 minutes. Remove the jars from the water and leave to cool on a wooden board. Store in a cool, dark place for up to 12 months. Refrigerate after opening.

COOK'S NOTE

This combination of pickled beans and leeks is delicious in salads (rinsed first if desired) or added to soups or casseroles. The same pickling solution and process can be used for other vegetables – try corn, asparagus, peas or zucchini (courgettes).

500 g (1 lb 2 oz) green beans, trimmed and cut into even lengths

500 g (1 lb 2 oz) yellow beans, trimmed and cut into even lengths

2 leeks, trimmed and thickly sliced

2 bay leaves

1 teaspoon black peppercorns

1 teaspoon yellow mustard seeds

115 g (4 oz/½ cup) caster (superfine) sugar

1 litre (34 fl oz/4 cups) white-wine vinegar

1 litre (34 fl oz/4 cups) water

PICKLED VANILLA PEACHES

Makes 2 litres (68 fl oz/8 cups)

2 kg (4 lb 6 oz) peaches
  (or nectarines)
460 g (1 lb/2 cups) caster
  (superfine) sugar
500 ml (17 fl oz/2 cups)
  apple-cider vinegar
3 vanilla beans, split
  lengthways and seeds
  scraped

1. Use a small, sharp knife to cut a shallow cross in the base
    of each peach. Drop the peaches into a pot of simmering
    water for 2 minutes to loosen their skins. Drain and transfer
    to a large bowl of iced water to cool.

2. Peel, halve and stone the peaches and put into warm
    sterilised jars.

3. Combine the sugar, vinegar and vanilla beans and seeds
    in a saucepan. Heat gently, stirring until the sugar dissolves,
    then bring to the boil. Cook for 10 minutes, or until syrupy.

4. Ladle the hot syrup over the peaches, making sure they are
    covered, and seal immediately. Store in a cool, dark place for
    up to 12 months. Refrigerate after opening. Serve warm or at
    room temperature with roasted meat such as lamb, pork or
    glazed ham.

PICKLED PEARS

Makes 1 litre (34 fl oz/4 cups)

345 g (12 oz/1½ cups) caster
    (superfine) sugar
500 ml (17 fl oz/2 cups)
    apple-cider vinegar
250 ml (8½ fl oz/1 cup) water
1 cinnamon stick
6 cloves
3 strips of orange zest
1 kg (2 lb 3 oz) small pears,
    peeled
2 rosemary sprigs

1. Combine the sugar, vinegar, water, spices and orange zest in a large saucepan. Place over low heat, stirring until the sugar dissolves, then increase the heat and boil for 5 minutes.

2. Add the whole pears and the rosemary sprigs, reduce the heat to low and simmer for 15–20 minutes, until the pears are just tender.

3. Use a slotted spoon to transfer the pears, spices, orange zest and rosemary to warm sterilised jars. Return the syrup to the boil, then remove it from the heat and pour over the pears, making sure they are covered. Seal the jars immediately. Store in a cool, dark place for up to 12 months. Refrigerate after opening.

COOK'S NOTE

While small pears work beautifully in this recipe, you can also use larger pears – just halve or quarter them lengthways and cut out the cores. Serve the pears as part of a cheese board or with pork.

SPICED PICKLED ORANGES WITH LIME

Makes 1 litre (34 fl oz/4 cups)

8 oranges, thickly sliced
460 g (1 lb/2 cups) caster (superfine) sugar
500 ml (17 fl oz/2 cups) white vinegar
juice of 4 limes
2 cinnamon sticks
6 cloves
1 teaspoon black peppercorns

1. Put the orange slices in a large saucepan and cover with water. Bring to the boil, then reduce the heat and simmer for 30 minutes, until the skin is tender. Drain, discarding the cooking water.

2. Combine the sugar, vinegar, lime juice and spices in the saucepan and place over low heat, stirring until the sugar dissolves. Bring to the boil and simmer for 5 minutes, or until syrupy. Add the orange slices and simmer over low heat for 30–40 minutes, until the skin is translucent.

3. Use a slotted spoon to transfer the hot orange slices into warm sterilised jars. Pour over the syrup, dividing the spices between the jars, and seal immediately. Store in a cool, dark place for up to 12 months. Refrigerate after opening. Serve with ham or chicken, or chop up and add to a tagine or casserole.

PRESERVING

PRESERVED LEMONS OR ORANGES

❧

sea salt flakes

lemons or small oranges,
  quartered

bay leaves (optional)

1 cinnamon stick (optional)

lemon or orange juice to
  cover

1. Sprinkle some salt into a sterilised jar (one with a plastic-lined lid, as salt is corrosive to metal). Pack lemon or orange wedges into the jar flesh-side down, sprinkling more salt over each layer, using 1 tablespoon of salt flakes for every lemon or orange. Keep packing in wedges and sprinkling on salt until the jar is full. You can add bay leaves to lemons or a cinnamon stick to oranges, if desired. Press down on the fruit to extract juice. Add enough juice to cover, if needed.

2. Wipe the neck of the jar with a clean cloth and seal immediately. Store in a cool, dark place for 2 months before using. Refrigerate after opening.

COOK'S NOTE

These gems are essential in any kitchen, being excellent for adding to casseroles, sauces, tagines and spice rubs, or simply for sprinkling over cooked fish. While preserved lemons are by far the most common, preserved oranges can be used in all the same ways – they simply taste a little sweeter and less bitter.

In fact, this recipe also works for cumquats, grapefruit or limes. If using cumquats, cut a cross in the stalk end of each cumquat, cutting halfway down the fruit, and open the fruit up slightly. If using grapefruit that are large, you might consider cutting into eighths. If using limes that are large, you can quarter them like lemons, or if they are small you can cut a cross in them in the same way as cumquats.

If the variety of lemons, oranges or grapefruit you are using have thick skins, boil them whole for 5 minutes before proceeding with the recipe. This helps to soften the fruit and accelerate the salt preservation.

When using the salted fruit, cut out the flesh and discard. Rinse the skins to remove excess salt and chop finely.

TOMATO PASSATA

tomatoes
salt

1. Boil ripe tomatoes in a large pot of salted water for
   3–5 minutes, until their skins split and they soften
   slightly. Scoop from the water and set aside to cool.

2. Pass the tomatoes through a food mill, discarding the solids.
   Strain the liquid if desired (if you prefer your passata extra
   smooth). Pour into warm sterilised jars or bottles and seal.

3. Stand the jars on a wire rack or trivet in the base of a deep
   pot. Fill the pot with water to cover the jars by at least 5 cm
   (2 in). Cover with a tight-fitting lid and slowly bring to the
   boil. Simmer for 45 minutes.

4. Remove the jars to a wooden board and leave to cool.
   Store in a cool, dark place for up to 12 months.
   Refrigerate after opening.

COOK'S NOTE

*All Italian families know that homemade passata is far
superior to store-bought, simply due to deliciously sweet
sun-ripened tomatoes and no preservatives! It's a family
tradition getting everyone together for bottling when there
is an abundance of tomatoes. The process is straightforward
– you just need a food mill, and a little patience as you pass
the tomatoes through the mill, bottle the purée, then boil the
bottles to ensure the passata won't spoil. When deciding how
much passata to make, it's handy to know that 1 kg (2 lb 3 oz)
of tomatoes makes approximately 700 ml (24 fl oz) of passata.*

PRESERVED TOMATOES

small tomatoes
red-wine vinegar

1. Use a small, sharp knife to cut a shallow cross in the base of each tomato. Drop the tomatoes, 2–3 at a time, into a saucepan of simmering water for 15 seconds. Scoop them out with a slotted spoon and drop into a large bowl of iced water while you continue to cook more tomatoes, then add them to the iced water.

2. Peel the tomatoes, then pack them into sterilised 1 litre (34 fl oz/4 cup) jars. Add 60 ml (2 fl oz/¼ cup) of vinegar to each jar and fill with boiling water, to cover the tomatoes. Seal immediately.

3. Stand the jars on a wire rack or trivet in the base of a deep pot. Fill the pot with boiling water to cover the jars by at least 5 cm (2 in). Cover with a tight-fitting lid and simmer for 45 minutes. Remove the jars from the water and leave to cool on a wooden board. Store in a cool, dark place for up to 12 months. Refrigerate after opening.

PRESERVED CAPSICUMS

1. Preheat a barbecue or chargrill pan to high and cook the capsicums for 10–15 minutes, turning, until blistered. (Alternatively, roast the capsicums in an oven heated to 200°C/180°C fan-forced (400°F/350°F) for 30 minutes.) Transfer the capsicums to a bowl, cover with plastic wrap and leave to cool (the steam helps loosen their skins).

2. Tear the capsicums in half, peel off their skins and remove the seeds. Pack the capsicum pieces into sterilised 1 litre (34 fl oz/4 cup) jars. Add 60 ml (2 fl oz/¼ cup) of vinegar to each jar then fill with boiling water, to cover the capsicums. Seal immediately.

3. Stand the jars on a wire rack or trivet in the base of a deep pot. Fill the pot with boiling water to cover the jars by at least 3 cm (1¼ in). Cover with a tight-fitting lid and simmer for 20 minutes. Remove the jars from the water and leave to cool on a wooden board. Store in a cool, dark place for up to 12 months. Refrigerate after opening.

COOK'S NOTE

When making preserved capsicums, you can use any colour capsicums, or even a mixture. Red and yellow capsicums are simply a little sweeter than green. Use them in almost any recipe calling for capsicum.

capsicums (bell peppers)
white-wine vinegar

Preserved
Tomatoes

Preserved Green
Mangoes with Lime

Preserved
Capsicums

PRESERVED GREEN MANGOES WITH LIME

Makes 750 ml (25 fl oz/3 cups)

1. Peel the mangoes and cut the flesh from the seeds in large pieces. (It is best to do this wearing gloves, as green mango causes skin irritation in some people.)

2. Combine the sugar, salt and water in a large saucepan and place over low heat, stirring until the sugar dissolves. Add the lime juice and mango pieces and bring to the boil. As soon as the syrup is boiling, remove the pan from the heat.

3. Use a slotted spoon to transfer the hot mango into warm sterilised jars. Return the syrup to the boil for 5 minutes.

4. Pour the hot syrup over the mango, making sure the mango is covered. Seal immediately.

5. Stand the jars on a wire rack or trivet in the base of a deep pot. Fill the pot with boiling water to cover the jars by at least 3 cm (1¼ in). Cover with a tight-fitting lid and simmer for 20 minutes. Remove the jars from the water and leave to cool on a wooden board. Store in a cool, dark place for up to 12 months. Refrigerate after opening.

COOK'S NOTE

Green mango is popular in Asian cuisine – it has a delightfully tart flavour and holds its shape well in salads. To use this preserved green mango, rinse off the pickling solution if desired, slice it and use as you would fresh.

1 kg (2 lb 3 oz) green mangoes
230 g (8 oz/1 cup) caster (superfine) sugar
2 teaspoons salt
1 litre (34 fl oz/4 cups) water
juice of 2 limes

GARLIC CONFIT

Makes 500 ml (17 fl oz/2 cups)

3 garlic bulbs
a few basil sprigs
extra-virgin olive oil
2 tablespoons white-wine
  vinegar

1. Separate the garlic into cloves. Put them (unpeeled) into
    a saucepan with the basil and pour over enough oil to just
    cover. Add the vinegar and bring to the boil, then simmer
    gently for 40 minutes, by which time the garlic will be soft.

2. Use a slotted spoon to transfer the hot garlic and basil into
    a warm sterilised jar, then pour over the hot oil. Seal and
    store in the refrigerator for up to 6 months. (The oil may
    congeal in the refrigerator, but this is not a sign of spoilage.)
    To use the garlic, squeeze the cloves from their skins and
    stir into mayonnaise, rub over bruschetta, spread over fish
    or stir through pasta or steamed vegetables. Use the oil
    in dressings or for cooking chicken.

COOK'S NOTE

*True confit is cooking and preserving an ingredient in its own
fat – hence the traditional French duck or goose confit. But the
term can be stretched to include the slow cooking of any food
in oil. While Mediterranean countries have been preserving in
olive oil for years, mainly due to the ready availability of the oil,
it is now known that some bacteria can survive under oil. Food
with low acidity is particularly susceptible, hence the addition
of vinegar to some foods. It is best to store confit preserves in
the refrigerator, and for a shorter time than other preserves.
It is also imperative that the food is submerged in oil – so when
you remove some of your confit from the jar and some of the
remaining confit becomes exposed, top up with a little extra
oil before resealing.*

ARTICHOKES IN OIL

Makes 1 litre (34 fl oz/4 cups)

10 globe artichokes

2 lemons

500 ml (17 fl oz/2 cups)
white-wine vinegar

750 ml (25 fl oz/3 cups)
extra-virgin olive oil

1 teaspoon black or white
peppercorns

1. Fill a large bowl with water and add the juice of 1 of the lemons. Working with 1 artichoke at a time, remove about half of its leaves. Cut off the top third of the artichoke and discard, and trim the stem to about 5–7 cm (2–2¾ in) long. Cut the artichoke in half lengthways and scoop out the hairy choke. Cut the remaining lemon in half and rub it over the cut surfaces of the artichoke, then drop the halves into the lemon water. The lemon prevents the artichoke from browning. Continue preparing the remaining artichokes.

2. Combine the vinegar and 1.5 litres (50 fl oz/6 cups) of water in a large saucepan and it bring to the boil. Add the artichokes and cover and simmer for 15–20 minutes, until tender.

3. Drain the artichokes, discarding the cooking liquid. Place the artichokes upside down on a few clean tea towels to allow excess liquid to drain from the leaves.

4. Heat the oil and peppercorns until shimmering. Pack the artichokes into warm sterilised jars and pour over the hot oil, making sure the artichokes are covered. Seal immediately. Store in the refrigerator for up to 6 months. (The oil may congeal in the refrigerator, but this is not a sign of spoilage.)

COOK'S NOTE

When preserving vegetables in oil, you can use the delicious left-over oil for frying or in salads once the vegetables are eaten.

ASPARAGUS AND WALNUTS IN OIL

Makes 500 ml (17 fl oz/2 cups)

1. Combine the vinegar and water in a saucepan and bring to the boil. Add the asparagus and walnuts, blanching for 1–2 minutes, until the asparagus is just tender. Drain, discarding the cooking liquid. Tip the asparagus and walnuts onto a clean tea towel or a layer of paper towel and pat dry.

2. Put the asparagus spears, standing up, into warm sterilised jars. Add the walnuts.

3. Heat the oil and peppercorns until shimmering, then pour them over the asparagus and walnuts, making sure they are covered. Seal immediately. Store in the refrigerator for up to 3 months. (The oil may congeal in the refrigerator, but this is not a sign of spoilage.)

COOK'S NOTE

You can also chargrill the asparagus after blanching to add a smoky flavour to this preserve. Serve the asparagus and walnuts on a platter or as a side dish, or mix through salad leaves.

250 ml (8½ fl oz/1 cup) white-wine vinegar

250 ml (8½ fl oz/1 cup) water

375 g (13 oz) asparagus, bases trimmed

100 g (3½ oz/1 cup) walnut halves

500 ml (17 fl oz/2 cups) extra-virgin olive oil

½ teaspoon black peppercorns

CAPSICUMS AND CHILLIES IN OIL

Makes 500 ml (17 fl oz/2 cups)

8 red capsicums
   (bell peppers)
8 long red chillies
juice of 2 lemons
3 oregano sprigs, leaves
   stripped from the stems
375 ml (12½ fl oz/1½ cups)
   extra-virgin olive oil

1. Preheat the oven to 200°C/180°C fan-forced (400°F/350°F). Put the whole capsicums and chillies on a large tray (lined with baking paper if desired) and bake for 30 minutes, until soft and charred. Transfer to a bowl, cover with plastic wrap and leave to cool (the steam helps loosen their skins).

2. Peel the capsicums and chillies and tear them in half. Remove the seeds. Tear the capsicum pieces in half again.

3. Layer the capsicum and chilli in warm sterilised jars, sprinkling with lemon juice and scattering with oregano leaves every so often. Heat the oil until shimmering and pour into the jars, making sure the capsicum and chilli are covered. Seal and store in the refrigerator for up to 3 months. (The oil may congeal in the refrigerator, but this is not a sign of spoilage.)

COOK'S NOTE

You can put these capsicums and chillies in salads or serve them as part of an antipasto platter.

TOMATOES AND TARRAGON IN OIL

Makes 1 litre (34 fl oz/4 cups)

1. Preheat the oven to 180°C/160°C fan-forced (350°F/320°F) and line an ovenproof dish or deep tray with baking paper. Add the tomatoes and scatter over the tarragon leaves. Season with salt and pepper and drizzle with the vinegar and 60 ml (2 fl oz/¼ cup) of the oil. Roast for 30 minutes.

2. Lift up the baking paper and use it to tip the hot tomatoes and their juices into warm sterilised jars. Cover with the remaining oil. Seal and store in the refrigerator for up to 1 month. (The oil may congeal in the refrigerator, but this is not a sign of spoilage.) Chop up and add to pasta sauces or stews (especially those with beef).

1 kg (2 lb 3 oz) tomatoes, halved
2 tarragon sprigs, leaves stripped from the stems
salt and pepper
60 ml (2 fl oz/¼ cup) red-wine vinegar
500 ml (17 fl oz/2 cups) extra-virgin olive oil

OLIVES

1. Cut a slit in each olive or prick 1 or 2 times with a skewer. Place in a plastic bucket and cover with water as salty as the sea, which is 240 g (8½ oz/1 cup) of salt to every 1 litre (34 fl oz/4 cups) of water. Leave for about 4 weeks, draining the olives and covering in fresh salted water each week. The salt draws out bitterness. Towards the end taste the olives regularly, as they can become too salty.

2. Once you like the flavour of the olives, drain off the brine. Transfer to sterilised jars and cover in olive oil or a weak brine (110 g/4 oz of salt to every 1 litre/34 fl oz/4 cups of water). Store in a cool, dark place for up to 12 months.

fresh black or green olives
salt
olive oil (optional)

PERILLA AND FETA ROLLS IN OIL

Makes 20 small rolls

1. Blanch the perilla leaves in boiling water for 1 second, then remove and transfer to a bowl of iced water. When the leaves are cool, drain them and pat dry with paper towel or a clean tea towel.

2. Cut the feta into 20 small rectangles. Place a piece of feta at the wide end of a perilla leaf. Roll the leaf around the feta, leaving the sides open, and place in a sterilised jar. Continue with the remaining leaves and feta, packing the rolls snugly into the jar. Sprinkle chilli flakes over each layer.

3. Pour enough oil over the rolls to cover them. Seal and store in the refrigerator for up to 2 weeks. (The oil may congeal in the refrigerator, but this is not a sign of spoilage.)

COOK'S NOTE

The herb perilla – also called shiso – has a unique herbaceous flavour, which is accentuated in this recipe. These rolls are delicious as part of a cheese platter or spread on toast. Labneh or goat's cheese can be used in place of feta. (Please note that while the recipe works for both red and green perilla leaves, if you use a mixture in the same jar they do discolour each other.)

20 large red or green perilla (shiso) leaves
200 g (7 oz) feta
½ teaspoon chilli flakes
extra-virgin olive oil

PRESERVED BERRIES

Makes 1 litre (34 fl oz/4 cups)

1 kg (2 lb 3 oz) berries of a
single variety or a mixture,
hulled as necessary
230 g (8 oz/1 cup) caster
(superfine) sugar

1. Put a layer of berries into a bowl or dish and sprinkle with
    some of the sugar. Top with another layer of berries and
    sugar. Repeat until all the berries and sugar have been used,
    then set aside at room temperature for 3 hours. The sugar
    will extract juice from the berries.

2. Transfer the mixture to a saucepan and gently bring to the
    boil, then immediately remove from the heat, ladle into
    warm sterilised jars and seal.

3. Stand the jars on a wire rack or trivet in the base of a deep
    pot. Fill the pot with boiling water to cover the jars by at
    least 3 cm (1¼ in). Cover with a tight-fitting lid and simmer
    for 20 minutes. Remove the jars from the water and leave
    to cool on a wooden board. Store in a cool, dark place for
    up to 12 months. Refrigerate after opening.

COOK'S NOTE

*When thinking of berries, we don't often think of preserving or
bottling them. While their texture softens, their flavour doesn't
change; in fact with some varieties it is enhanced. Preserved
berries can be served on top of ice-cream or yoghurt, cooked
in pies, or added to cake or muffin batters.*

PRESERVED PEACHES WITH PASSIONFRUIT

Makes 2 litres (68 fl oz/8 cups)

1. Use a small, sharp knife to cut a shallow cross in the base of each peach. Drop the peaches into a large saucepan of simmering water for 2 minutes to loosen their skins. Drain and transfer to a bowl of iced water to cool.

2. Peel, halve and stone the peaches (see Cook's note). Combine the sugar and 1 litre (34 fl oz/4 cups) of water in a large saucepan and place over low heat, stirring until the sugar dissolves. Bring to the boil, then stir in the passionfruit pulp. Add the peach halves and return to the boil, then remove from the heat.

3. Use a slotted spoon to transfer the hot peaches to warm sterilised jars. Pour over the passionfruit syrup, covering the peaches. Seal immediately.

4. Stand the jars on a wire rack or trivet in the base of a deep pot. Fill the pot with boiling water to cover the jars by at least 3 cm (1¼ in). Cover with a tight-fitting lid and simmer for 20 minutes. Remove the jars from the water and leave to cool on a wooden board. Store in a cool, dark place for up to 12 months. Refrigerate after opening.

1 kg (2 lb 3 oz) peaches
170 g (6 oz/¾ cup) caster (superfine) sugar
250 ml (8½ fl oz/1 cup) passionfruit pulp

COOK'S NOTE

This recipe can be made with either freestone or clingstone peaches. You can remove the stones from clingstone peaches by cutting and twisting the peach to open it, then using a teaspoon to scoop out the stone, taking a small amount of flesh with it. When stoning peaches you may like to scrape the red flesh from their cavities, as it tends to darken once preserved.

PRESERVED PLUMS WITH ALMONDS

Makes 2 litres (68 fl oz/8 cups)

1. Use a fork to prick the skins of the plums to prevent them from bursting.

2. Combine the sugar and water in a large saucepan and place over low heat, stirring until the sugar dissolves. Bring to the boil, then add the plums and almonds. Allow the syrup to return to the boil, then remove from the heat.

3. Use a slotted spoon to transfer the hot plums and almonds to warm sterilised jars. Pour over the syrup, covering the plums and almonds. Seal immediately.

4. Stand the jars on a wire rack or trivet in the base of a deep pot. Fill the pot with boiling water to cover the jars by at least 3 cm (1¼ in). Cover with a tight-fitting lid and simmer for 20 minutes. Remove the jars from the water and leave to cool on a wooden board. Store in a cool, dark place for up to 12 months. Refrigerate after opening.

1 kg (2 lb 3 oz) plums of any variety
230 g (8 oz/1 cup) caster (superfine) sugar
1.5 litres (50 fl oz/6 cups) water
45 g (1½ oz/½ cup) flaked almonds

PRESERVED APPLES WITH CINNAMON

Makes 1.5 litres (50 fl oz/6 cups)

juice of 1 lemon
1 kg (2 lb 3 oz) apples
230 g (8 oz/1 cup) caster
 (superfine) sugar
3 cinnamon sticks

1. Fill a large bowl with water and add the lemon juice. Peel the apples, cut them into halves or quarters, and cut out the cores. Drop the apples into the lemon water to prevent them from browning.

2. Combine the sugar and 1 litre (34 fl oz/4 cups) of water in a large saucepan and place over low heat, stirring until the sugar dissolves. Bring to the boil. Drain the apples and add to the syrup with the cinnamon sticks. Simmer for 5 minutes.

3. Use a slotted spoon to transfer the hot apples to warm sterilised jars, making sure there is a cinnamon stick in each jar. Pour over the syrup, to cover the apples. Seal immediately.

4. Stand the jars on a wire rack or trivet in the base of a deep pot. Fill the pot with boiling water to cover the jars by at least 3 cm (1¼ in). Cover with a tight-fitting lid and simmer for 20 minutes. Remove the jars from the water and leave to cool on a wooden board. Store in a cool, dark place for up to 12 months. Refrigerate after opening.

PRESERVED PEARS WITH CARDAMOM

Makes 1.5 litres (50 fl oz/6 cups)

juice of 1 lemon
1 kg (2 lb 3 oz) pears
230 g (8 oz/1 cup) caster
  (superfine) sugar
2 teaspoons cardamom
  pods, cracked

1. Fill a large bowl with water and add the lemon juice. Peel the pears, cut them into halves or quarters, and cut out the cores. Drop the pears into the lemon water to prevent them from browning.

2. Combine the sugar and 1 litre (34 fl oz/4 cups) of water in a large saucepan and place over low heat, stirring until the sugar dissolves. Bring to the boil. Drain the pears, then add them to the syrup with the cardamom pods to simmer for 5 minutes.

3. Use a slotted spoon to transfer the hot pears to warm sterilised jars. Pour over the syrup, covering the pears. Seal immediately.

4. Stand the jars on a wire rack or trivet in the base of a deep pot. Fill the pot with boiling water to cover the jars by at least 3 cm (1¼ in). Cover with a tight-fitting lid and simmer for 20 minutes. Remove the jars from the water and leave to cool on a wooden board. Store in a cool, dark place for up to 12 months. Refrigerate after opening.

PRESERVED CHERRIES

Makes 2 litres (68 fl oz/8 cups)

345 g (12 oz/1½ cups) caster
  (superfine) sugar
2 star anise
4 strips of orange zest
500 ml (17 fl oz/2 cups) water
1 kg (2 lb 3 oz) cherries,
  stems removed

1. Combine the sugar, star anise, orange zest and water in
    a large saucepan and place over low heat, stirring until
    the sugar dissolves. Bring to the boil then add the whole
    cherries. Allow the mixture to return to the boil then remove
    from the heat.

2. Use a slotted spoon to transfer the hot cherries to warm
    sterilised jars. Pour over the syrup, to cover the cherries.
    Seal immediately.

3. Stand the jars on a wire rack or trivet in the base of a deep
    pot. Fill the pot with boiling water to cover the jars by at
    least 3 cm (1¼ in). Cover with a tight-fitting lid and simmer
    for 20 minutes. Remove the jars from the water and leave
    to cool on a wooden board. Store in a cool, dark place for
    up to 12 months. Refrigerate after opening.

COOK'S NOTE

*The cherries can be stoned using a cherry or olive stoner
if preferred.*

ACKNOWLEDGEMENTS

Firstly, thank you to the many regional producers who opened their farms to us for photography for this book and who supplied some of the magnificent produce, particularly Alf from Sorbello Heirloom Tomatoes; Brackenridge Berries; Waitui and Waitui Community Garden; and the Uniting Church Community Garden, Cundletown.

Thank you to Tracy Rutherford for allowing us to choose props from her substantial prop room for the food shoot.

To Jane Collins, food stylist, for transforming the preserves into beautiful images, but most of all for her continued friendship and advice.

Thank you to photographer Natasha Milne for her eye and hard work on the farm shoot.

Acknowledgement must also go to Paul McNally and the rest of the Hardie Grant team for their hard work and vision, particularly Meelee Soorkia, Mark Campbell, Rachel Pitts, Kate Barraclough and Jeremy Simons.

Meredith would like to thank Mandy – the talented 'woman in the kitchen', who crafts such deliciousness – and also her mother and grandmother, for their hand-me-down lessons and learning.

From Mandy to Meredith – thank you for the gardening inspiration and the helpful advice with growing my produce!

Finally, thank you to our beautiful families for their never-ending support, encouragement and advice.

INDEX

Published in 2015 by Hardie Grant Books

Hardie Grant Books (Australia)
Ground Floor, Building 1
658 Church Street
Richmond, Victoria 3121
www.hardiegrant.com.au

Hardie Grant Books (UK)
5th & 6th Floors
52–54 Southwark Street
London SE1 1UN
www.hardiegrant.co.uk

Copyright text © Mandy Sinclair and Meredith Kirton
Copyright garden photography © Natasha Milne
Copyright food photography © Jeremy Simons
Copyright design © Hardie Grant Books

A Cataloguing-in-Publication entry is available from the catalogue
of the National Library of Australia at www.nla.gov.au
The Produce Companion
ISBN 978 1 74270 919 2

Publishing director: Paul McNally
Senior editor: Meelee Soorkia
Editor: Rachel Pitts
Design manager: Mark Campbell
Designer: Kate Barraclough
Garden photographer: Natasha Milne
Food photographer: Jeremy Simons
Stylist: Jane Collins
Illustrator: Heather Menzies
Production Manager: Todd Rechner

Colour reproduction by Splitting Image Colour Studio
Printed and bound in China by 1010 Printing International Limited